EXTREME
ENCOUNTERS

Library of Congress Control Number: 2001094933

ISBN: 1-931686-00-9

Printed in Singapore

Typeset in Officina and Alt Gothic

Designed by Bryn Ashburn

Photo Credits:

Shark (page 10 and cover): © Jeffrey L. Rotman/CORBIS
Tornado (page 36 and cover): © Getty Images
Skull and crossbones (page 66 and cover): © Getty Images
Prison bars (page 90): © Getty Images
Blow-dryer (page 120): © Getty Images
Frightened Man (page 144 and cover): © CORBIS

Distributed in North America by Chronicle Books
85 Second Street
San Francisco, CA 94105

10 9 8 7 6 5 4 3 2 1

Quirk Books
215 Church Street
Philadelphia, PA 19106
www.quirkbooks.com

EXTREME
ENCOUNTERS

How It Feels to Be Drowned
in Quicksand, Shredded by Piranhas,
Swept Up in a Tornado, and Dozens
of Other Unpleasant Experiences . . .

by Greg Emmanuel

QUIRK BOOKS
PHILADELPHIA

CONTENTS

I. WHEN ANIMALS ATTACK

II. THE GREAT OUTDOORS

III. SOMEBODY GET A DOCTOR!

IV. CRIME AND PUNISHMENT

V. EVERYDAY MISHAPS

VI. GOING TO EXTREMES

INTRODUCTION

There are certain themes of which the interest is all-absorbing, but which are too entirely horrible for the purposes of legitimate fiction.

—EDGAR ALLAN POE, *THE PREMATURE BURIAL*, 1850

What was it like? Did it hurt? What could you see? And then what happened? These are the kinds of questions I've been asked since one fateful evening at the end of 2000, when an unexpected collision sent my '88 Ford Escort tumbling down New York's Saw Mill Parkway.

It was easily the most horrific experience of my life. At the time of impact, my girlfriend Jessica and I were just outside of New York City, heading north to her parents' house in Connecticut. It was nearly 9:00 on a clear, crisp fall evening, and the parkway's many serpentine twists lay before us. I turned up the volume on the radio, forcing myself to stay alert. Jessica was beginning to nod off in the passenger seat, and our two-year-old cat, Henry, was dozing on her lap.

The collision came out of nowhere. We were hit hard from behind and our car went airborne. Following the thunderous impact, there was an eerie silence as we lost all notions of time and space. Then, suddenly, we smashed into the ground and rolled in a deafening symphony of twisted metal and broken glass. The car went around and around at least three times. We landed upside down on the other side of the highway, now facing oncoming traffic (and a number of very skillful drivers who managed to avoid us). When you're in a serious accident, the ordinary passing of seconds seems to feel like an eternity. There was nothing to do but wait for "the end," whatever the end would be.

Eventually, our vehicle slowed to a stop. Jessica managed to tell me she was okay. Miraculously, I felt like I was okay, too. I remember trying to wiggle my toes—I figured if I could wiggle my toes, then I couldn't possibly be paralyzed. But then I realized my hand was sitting in a pool of blood. And as soon as I saw the blood, I felt the pain—searing and hot.

Since that night, I've been asked about the accident many times. People who hear the tale exhibit a wide range of responses—everything from shock and anxiety to repulsion and relief. (Most people also ask about Henry the cat, who must have jumped out of one of the windows during the crash. Remarkably he was found, safe and sound, another fifteen days later—a saga for a different book.)

The more I've told this story, the more I realize that people find these kinds of horror stories fascinating (or "all-absorbing," as Poe puts it). And why not? When I describe my car accident—or when a journalist like Jon Krakauer describes a disastrous expedition to the top of Mount Everest, or Sebastian Junger recounts a savage nor'easter that overwhelms a small fishing boat—the reader can share vicariously in the experience without any risk of dying, bleeding, freezing, drowning, or even breaking a sweat. We can experience the heights and depths of the human experience, without ever putting ourselves seriously at risk.

Now, if that's your idea of a good time, you've opened the right book. Perhaps the accident gave me an unhealthy fascination with my own mortality. I'll admit that I became more curious about life-or-death situations. How much worse would my accident have been, for example, if I'd been driving in a NASCAR rally instead of on the Saw Mill Parkway? (Jump to page 162 if you need to know immediately.) What would it have been like to be revived by a defibrillator? (That info can be found on page 67.) From there, a slightly overactive imagination took over. I wondered how it would feel to be stranded in a desert, to skydive, to go without sleep for ninety-six hours, to sail over Niagara Falls in a barrel. And the outline of this book slowly began to take shape.

Researching *Extreme Encounters* led me to some very unusual sources (my librarian probably contemplated calling the police after I borrowed books with titles like *History of Torture*, *How We Die*, and *White Death*—all in the same visit). I interviewed people as disparate as a trauma doctor, a woman struck by lightning, and a skydiving instructor. And over the course of these conversations, I learned a number of fascinating facts: A piranha can go from open mouth to clenched teeth in less than five milliseconds. A proper hanging will kill a person by snapping the spine, not by cutting off the air supply. A .22 slug will bounce around the inside of the human body like a pinball. And if you're ever caught in an avalanche, a few drops of saliva can save your life.

The "extreme encounters" in this book are divided into six different sections. Part I describes encounters with a number of different animals—from tiny fire ants to a massive grizzly bear. Part II covers a wide range of outdoor scenarios like tornadoes, quicksand, avalanches, and frostbite. Part III features medical emergencies of all different kinds (including the always-underestimated kidney stone, which can be as tiny as a tomato seed but still wreak incredible havoc on your urinary system).

Part IV is devoted to crime and punishment (yes, there really was such a thing called the "Chinese water torture," but it was invented in sixteenth-century Italy by a lawyer named Hippolytus de Marsiliis). Part V describes a number of common accidents and everyday mishaps (and I really do mean everyday—statistics show that someone somewhere in the United States will be struck by lightning before today is over). Part VI is called "Going to Extremes" and concerns situations that many people will voluntarily participate in—like going nine rounds with a heavyweight boxer, for example, or jumping out of an airplane. But trust me: voluntary participation doesn't make these situations any less frightening.

To achieve an even greater degree of verisimilitude, all of the tales in this book have been written in the second person—so *you* chill to the numbing effects of frostbite, *you* hear the earsplitting roar of a tornado, and *you* feel the stomach-lurching drop of an elevator free fall. This unusual narrative point of view is partly in homage to my favorite childhood books—the *Choose Your Own Adventure* series. But unlike those books—where your fate in the story depended on choices made by the reader—your fates in these stories have been pre-determined by the author. And I should warn you: the outcomes are not always pleasant.

But don't worry about it. Indulge your fantasies. Satisfy your morbid curiosities. Learn something. And have a little fun. (Sorry, Edgar, but these directives sound like the point of "legitimate fiction"—at least to me.) Yes, it is a jungle out there—and if you want to steel yourself against the very worst that can happen, the stories in *Extreme Encounters* are an excellent place to begin. Enjoy them in a place that's very comfortable . . . and very safe.

PART I

WHEN ANIMALS ATTACK

fire ant picnic

I was stung all up and down my legs, and I had welts all over them and on my side. They burned for days. I never had such an experience in all my life.

—MARION BERNHARDT, 77, ASSAULTED BY FIRE ANTS IN WEST PALM BEACH, FLORIDA, 1994

It's a beautiful summer afternoon under a clear Alabama sky, and you and your sister are driving into the countryside for a picnic. You park the car near a secluded pasture and then follow a trail along a river until you reach a sunny, grassy clearing. You unpack your lunch, arranging Tupperware containers, bottles of Evian, and a bag of Cheddarwursts (your favorite!) in the shade of a small hickory tree. Your sister realizes that you've left the bug spray in the car and decides to run back for it. After all, the woods are full of pesky critters.

As she sets off, you lean back against the tree, enjoying the solitude and stretching out in the grass. Your left heel comes to rest against a small mound of dirt—probably the buried remains of someone else's picnic, you figure. But this innocuous-looking mound is actually home to a quarter of a million fire ants and their queen, who is busy producing 1,600 eggs per day.

Forget what you've heard: size really doesn't matter. Only as big as a pencil point, the tiny *Solenopsis wagneri*—or red imported fire ant—will wreak havoc and even kill. Indigenous to Brazil and Argentina, it is believed that these poisonous ants smuggled themselves into the United States around 1930 by hiding in cargo ships. Today red imported fire ants live throughout the South and are rapidly spreading north and west like they have some kind of miniature manifest destiny.

Consider Marion Bernhardt, a seventy-seven-year-old woman in West Palm Beach, Florida, who entered the hospital for intestinal surgery. A few hours after the doctors finished her operation, Bernhardt complained of a burning sensation near her incision. The nurses assured her it was just the result of her medication wearing off—but when they finally pulled back the blankets, they discovered that her body (and, particularly, the fresh incision) were swarming with ants.

Marion Bernhardt wasn't even asking for trouble, but you've just placed your foot on an entire nest of ants—a surefire way to invoke their wrath. Using a combination of pheromones and low-frequency sounds, hundreds of thousands of fire ants can mobilize in less than ten seconds. They perceive your foot as a threat to the colony, and within moments your sneakers and socks are being marched across by an army of ants (not to be confused with army ants, which, thankfully, are still confined to tropical and subtropical areas).

Fire ants do not have eyes, so your attackers guide themselves to the exposed skin of your legs with the help of two tiny antennae on the front of their heads. Also protruding from the head is a small mandible—a pincer-like structure with sharp serrated edges. The ants use this tool to do everything from building to biting.

The first sensation you feel is like a tiny pinprick. The pinch fades quickly but it is immediately replaced by a severe burning, as if someone's lit a match and touched it to your calf. In actuality, one ant's mandible has pierced your skin. Scores of tiny nerve receptors relay an impulse from the point of impact to the spinal cord, which your brain quickly translates as a pinch. But the fire ant is not finished: Like an Olympic gymnast, it swings its abdomen between its legs and inserts a stinger into your flesh, injecting a venom made predominantly of an alkaloid called *piperidine*. This substance is the "fire" in fire ant—and it's toxic enough to kill numerous cells at the site of the injection.

One bite is unpleasant enough, but the red fire ants attack *en masse*. Hundreds of ants are evacuating the colony, swarming up your legs, and piercing your skin with their mandibles. Each ant stings repeatedly, up to six or seven times. The burning sensation caused by hundreds of bites is agonizing—like your legs are on fire.

All of this transpires in a matter of seconds. You look down and realize your legs are swarming with bugs. You desperately try to swat them off—but every handful that you swat away are replaced by hundreds more, and making contact with your hand has just given them another surface to infest. You shout for your sister to come back. You reach for your water bottle and try to douse the bugs with Evian, but by this point you'd need a fire hose to wash the ants away.

Fire ants are not necessarily deadly. If you managed to brush the ants off and run away from the colony, all you'd have to deal with is an hour of lingering discomfort, followed by the formation of hundreds of small blisters at the site of each sting. In a day or two, these blisters would become unsightly white, infected pustules. Unfortunately, you won't live long enough to see what these pustules look like.

In quick succession: Your eyes begin to swell. Your mouth and tongue feel thick and swollen. It is difficult to breathe; you are sweating profusely and feeling nauseated. Your mouth makes an odd whistling noise as you struggle to inhale. You are experiencing a rare but severe condition known as *anaphylaxis*, an intense reaction to an allergen (in this case, the fire ant's poison). The first symptom is *angioedema*, the swelling of the mucous membranes of the eyes and mouth. This symptom is usually followed by *laryngeal edema*, the swelling of the throat. And the whistling noise you hear is *stridor*—the sound of the impending closure of your airway.

Anaphylaxis is followed closely by full *anaphylactic shock*: Your body struggles to supply enough oxygen to your tissue and organs, but you quickly fall unconscious. Your blood vessels open wide and your artery walls expand in a last-ditch effort to continue circulation. It's too late. Just a minute or two later, your sister comes bounding down the trail, bug spray in hand, only to discover your dead body completely covered with ants.

snake in the grass

I couldn't believe my eyes when it charged at me. I froze for almost ten seconds, and that was enough to let the snake tangle itself around me.

—LUCAS SIBANDA, ATTACKED BY A PYTHON IN SOUTH AFRICA, 2001

You've been stuck working overtime for the past three days and Princess, your golden retriever, is not very pleased. When you arrive home late Friday evening, your slippers are chewed to pieces, there's a conspicuous wet stain on the carpet, and there are deep scratch marks on the back of the door, as if Princess has tried to claw her way out. You know this is your own fault—dogs obviously need lots of attention and exercise, and you've been neglecting your responsibilities as a pet owner.

So the next morning, you bring Princess into the backyard for a game of Frisbee toss. It's a gorgeous day in Toledo, Ohio, and playing with the dog is keeping your mind off work. Princess catches every throw and obediently runs back with the Frisbee. Then you try to throw a long one and snap your wrist a little too hard; the Frisbee goes sailing over a fence and lands in your neighbor's yard. Princess doesn't want to trespass (good dog!) so you hop the fence to get the Frisbee yourself.

It's not so easy to find. The last time you saw your neighbor mow his lawn was five years ago, and some of the weeds are higher than your knees. Ahead of you, there's a shuffling in the grass, and you naturally assume it's a bird or squirrel. But then something strikes your calf, and it feels like two small nails have been pounded into your leg. You look down and can't believe your eyes—it appears that a python has clamped its jaws around your ankle.

Toledo isn't known for its wide variety of untamed snakes, but you've managed to stumble across one of the worst kinds. Constrictors squeeze the life out of an animal before beginning the slow process of digesting it. And these suckers are big: The mightiest of the constrictors is the reticulated python, which can grow in excess of thirty feet and weigh almost three hundred pounds.

Reticulated pythons live in Southeast Asia and generally feed upon medium-sized mammals like pigs and goats. But they're not afraid to move higher up the food chain; every year, a handful of humans are attacked by pythons, and a few wind up dead. Take, for example, Ee Heng Chuan, a twenty-nine-year-old Malaysian rubber tapper who was attacked in his own backyard; when police found Chuan, the python was still trying to swallow him, and it took four rounds from an M-16 rifle to stop the reptile.

Perhaps more unsettling is the number of python attacks that don't occur in the wilds of Malaysia, but rather in Illinois or Colorado or even New York City. Many eccentrics seem to enjoy keeping pythons as house pets; it's estimated that tens of thousands of giant snakes are in captivity. And if you think Princess doesn't like being stuck in the house all day, imagine how a three-hundred-pound snake accustomed to living in the jungle might feel. Wild animals placed in suburban environments will always escape if given the opportunity—and after one week of slithering through a landscape of paved highways and strip malls, this particular snake is very confused, very agitated, and very hungry. It's only natural that such a creature might pause to rest in your neighbor's yard, where the untamed weeds and grass offer some semblance of home.

Of course, you don't know any of that. You just know that there's a thirty-foot snake in your neighbor's backyard, and its jaw is clamped around the bottom of your leg. Pythons generally avoid preying on humans because we're too damn hard to swallow—but this one is attracted to you because it has picked up the scent of your dog. Although its teeth contain no venom, the bite on your calf achieves its intended effect, which is to startle and disorient you (if you were a smaller animal, you'd be in shock by now). Before you realize what's happening, the snake has already coiled its body between your legs. You try to pull away and nearly succeed, but the snake swivels its body at the last moment, tripping you to the ground. You collapse amid the tall weeds.

Although big snakes are sometimes perceived as slow and slothful, they can strike quickly when there's food to be had. As you scramble backward, the python uses the opportunity to loop over and under your body, ensnaring you like a net. Its skin has a cool, almost lifeless feel; it's covered in overlapping scales made of a protein called *keratin* that locks in moisture. The snake's head is narrow with bright orange eyes and a flickering tongue; you strike it with your fist, to no avail. Then you try to scream for help—maybe your neighbor will hear you— but your body is so tense that even your vocal cords fail you; all that comes out is a weak squawk.

Experts would say you have two chances for survival. If the snake was small enough, you might untangle its thick coils from your body—but this animal outweighs you by more than a hundred pounds. A much more likely possibility is that the snake will eventually realize you're too big to swallow whole; when this happens, it will simply slither away. Unfortunately, this particular snake has spent the last week in suburbia without a meal, so you look like Thanksgiving dinner. The snake may sense it can't swallow all of you, but it certainly wants to try.

The snake circles your body using a process called rectilinear motion.

The python presses its scales into your leg and pushes against those scales with its ribs to slither its massive body around. The body is sequentially lifted, anchored, and pushed forward by resistance against the scales—which gives the impression of effortlessly sliding forward.

Your first instinct is to hold your breath, to store a good supply of air in your lungs. But of course this does nothing except make you feel weak. The python moves around your midsection and circles your chest. As you exhale, the snake coils tighter around your body, and you feel tension around your ribs like you're wearing a tight corset. With each subsequent exhalation, the snake tightens its grip like a living vise. You start to sweat, your pulse quickens, and your blood pressure rises.

Because of the python's crushing hold on your chest, your diaphragm can't contract and your chest cavity can't expand—so there's no air flowing into your oxygen-starved lungs. Your ribs are cracking, but you don't even notice the pain because you're too busy struggling to breathe. The blood in your veins is quickly filling with unwanted carbon dioxide. This condition is called *hypercarbia*; as you struggle desperately to get air into your lungs, you feel confused and a little sleepy, like a fog is clouding your thoughts. Soon after, you lose consciousness. As the level of carbon dioxide continues to climb, your heartbeat turns abnormal and then eventually stops altogether. A few moments later, all electrical activity in your brain ceases.

Meanwhile, some fifty feet away, Princess finally breaks your "no trespassing" rule and wriggles under the fence. By the time she catches up to you, the python has unhinged its jaws so that it can fit your body in its mouth (the snake has no trouble swallowing your head and neck, but won't make it past your broad shoulders). Princess and the python exchange a tense stare; your dog barks a few times, but quickly grows fidgety and then runs off to find something more fun to play with.

And the python—recognizing an easily digestible meal when it sees one—gives up on you and quickly slithers after her.

shark! who goes there?

Sharks don't even like the taste of humans, with all our bones. It's just unfortunate that when they take a taste, with one or two bites, the bites can be fatal.

—RODNEY FOX, SHARK-ATTACK VICTIM TURNED SHARK EXPERT,
AUSTRALIA, 2000

You're snorkeling near the shore, floating gently on the surface of the water, mesmerized by the colorful fish that are passing underneath you. It's the third day of your vacation in Australia, and you're exploring a small coral reef near Adelaide. Marine biology has always been a hobby of yours, and for years you've studied fascinating reports about Adelaide's abundant marine wildlife. Now that you're finally here, you're certainly not disappointed. The bay is rife with seahorses and yellow-tail scad, and at one point you see a moray eel that is nearly three feet long.

But then—seemingly all at once—these creatures disappear. You sense a strange calmness in the sea—even the reeds and plants seem eerily still. You're contemplating the beauty of this tranquility when something from below the water hits you extraordinarily hard.

Shark attacks don't just happen in the movies. In the year 2000, there were seventy-nine confirmed attacks around the world that resulted in ten deaths. More than two-thirds of the attacks occurred in North America (where there's a lot of ocean recreation). But thanks to your interest in marine biology, you know that fears of a shark attack are relatively unfounded (you're actually thirty times more likely to be struck by lightning).

Tiger and bull sharks are man-eaters, but the biggest threat to humans is the great white. Averaging fifteen feet long and three thousand pounds, this formidable fish has no natural predator except for other great whites and humans. It attacks hard and fast and with unimaginable force. Then there are those jaws. They make other creatures' so-called mouths look rudimentary. The great white will lift its snout prior to striking and drop its lower jaw in a menacing pose that increases the bite force and the efficiency of its teeth. That average bite force is twenty tons per square inch (the same as a bullet leaving the barrel of a gun) and the teeth are three inches long, wicked sharp, and serrated like a fine steak knife. They cut through bone like it's butter, and the shark's numerous large teeth are backed up by a second row of chompers ready to replace a defective tooth—like marching phalanxes of slicing and dicing.

When you first encounter the shark, you're floating in about seven feet of water (the majority of shark attacks occur in shallow water, where sharks may be confined by low tide, or near steep drop-offs, where prey tends to congregate). As you float on the surface of the water, you bear an uncanny resemblance to the great white's favorite meal: a sea lion. The first blow feels like you've been hit by a freight train; the impact throws you clear out of the water, and you splash back down disoriented. This was actually the shark's first attempt to bite you, and you're lucky that its jaws didn't make contact.

As you float to the surface, trying to regain your bearings, you feel a crushing pressure clamp down on your right side. Survival instincts kick in and your mind registers the pressure of the bite, but no pain. It feels as if your insides have been shifted toward the left side of your body. In fact, the great white has succeeded in its second attempt to bite you, and its massive jaws have removed a substantial section of your torso.

Now you are beginning to understand what's happening—but it's still hard to accept that you are actually being attacked by a shark. This thought is quickly replaced by the urgent realization that you need air. As you flail to get to the surface, you notice that the once crystal-clear water is now clouded red with your blood.

Most shark attack victims agree that the most overwhelming part of the experience is not the pain, but rather the sheer horror of the situation. Your endorphins help you deal with the pain, but your heart is racing and you know you have to get away from this bloodthirsty predator. You manage to keep your head out of the water and take a long deep breath. The rush of oxygen, which travels into your lungs and is delivered to cells throughout your body, momentarily calms you.

The shore is fairly close, but you can't move well enough to swim. Right now, all of your energy is devoted to staying afloat and scream-ing for help. As blood spills from the wound in your side, your heart beats faster to keep your circulation on track.

Fortunately, the great white has already moved on. The shark simply got a taste of you and realized you weren't a blubber-rich seal. (Most great white attacks on humans involve just one bite.) You are now los-ing a lot of blood, but your screams have alerted your friends on the beach, who swim out to help you. Once you're safely on shore, you look down and see a huge, bloody mess.

The wound is ghastly, but amazingly missed damaging your heart, lungs, and major arteries. You slip in and out of consciousness, but there is just enough time to get you to a hospital and stop the bleed-ing. It'll take a few hundred stitches to sew you up, but at least you'll live.

Snorkeling again, however, is another matter. And the possibility of ever watching *Jaws* again is definitely out of the question.

maul of the wild

I just knew she was going to kill me. [She was] chewing and biting on me, holding me down and biting, but not jerking. She chewed on my hand the longest. Every time she bit it felt like she was crushing it. It hurt bad, really bad. She was pretty loud and was growling and bellowing the whole time.

—ED HIGBIE, ATTACKED BY A GRIZZLY BEAR IN THE TETON WILDERNESS NEAR YELLOWSTONE NATIONAL PARK, 1990

This is not a bluff charge: A 550-pound female grizzly is upon you in mere seconds, slamming you to the ground like a defensive back for the New York Giants. All you see is a blur of fur—and then you're face down in the dirt, choking on the pungent breath of your attacker, which reeks of rotting meat. You struggle to your feet but the grizzly clamps her jaws around your torso, hoisting you off the ground. You're six feet tall and weigh 190 pounds—not petite by any definition—but the mighty grizzly shakes you like a rag doll.

There is nothing predictable about a grizzly bear—except maybe its massive size and uncanny ability to kill you. The grizzly of North America is called *Ursus horribilis*, and this species is aptly named. Each one weighs between 250 and 750 pounds and is basically indestructible; when a bear attacks a human, the results are almost always gruesome.

There are about 35,000 grizzlies living throughout North America, but only about 1,200 can be found south of Canada. Most of these roam in or around Yellowstone and Glacier National Parks. But for all the hype that bear attacks receive, only nine people have been killed by grizzlies in the United States since 1980. And serious maulings add just fifty-seven additional tally marks to the body count.

With these reassuring odds on your side, you confidently take off on the Yellowstone River Trail for an overnight stay in the backwoods. Park rangers report that there have been no recent bear sightings in the area, but you still take the necessary precautions, like making plenty of noise as you walk along the trail and clapping your hands as you round blind curves. As you ascend the trail, circling around a large boulder, you spot a large grizzly about one hundred feet up the trail. No reason to panic, you figure—a few loud noises and some careful backstepping should deliver you from harm's way. Then a soft rustling in the leaves causes you to look over your shoulder, and you see two small bear cubs eating blackberries. Now, this *is* a reason to panic: By unwittingly walking between a sow and her cubs, you have positioned yourself as a threat—and a startled grizzly becomes very angry very quickly. Her charge is fierce and lightning-fast—a grizzly can cover a distance of fifty yards in three seconds.

You try to protect yourself by hitting the bear with your fists, but this only further provokes your attacker. For the record: A grizzly bear has six pointed cutting teeth, two strong, sharp, curved canines, and molar teeth that are superior blades. When you raise a hand to the bear's salivating mouth, the appendage is severed at the wrist bone.

You are now aware that you are losing copious amounts of blood—yet it's not nearly as painful as you'd expect, because the sympathetic division of your autonomic nervous system has been activated. This helps your body respond to stress by directing the adrenal glands to secrete two hormones: *epinephrine* (adrenaline) and *norepinephrine* (noradrenaline). In concert, these chemicals accelerate your heartbeat, increase muscle tension, raise your blood pressure, and divert blood flow from the internal organs and skin to the brain and muscles. All of these biological responses make you less sensitive to pain, because your body is otherwise preoccupied.

Once the grizzly perceives that she has killed you (and thus ended the threat to her cubs) she stops shaking you and backs away. Drawing on energy supplied by the adrenaline, you manage to rise to your feet. Big mistake—you should have just played dead. The bear swipes again, this time at your torso, and your ribs snap like a bundle of dry twigs. As you fall to your knees, the bear puts your head in its mouth—an absurdly unnecessary, instinctive movement *to prevent you from biting back*. Blood is streaming from your head and pooling in front of your eyes. Another swipe to the chest pierces your rib cage and punctures a lung; your breathing becomes labored as air escapes through a hole in your chest. Your facial and neck muscles contort and throb as they work to replace the oxygen escaping from your lungs. Luckily, you feel strangely detached from everything that is happening. Victims of grizzly attacks describe the experience as "numbness," often accompanied by matter-of-fact thoughts like "I am going to die today."

Once you finally stop moving, the grizzly leaves you alone, gathers up her two cubs, and resumes her walk down the trail. But it's too late for you. Blood flow to the brain is slowing and you feel consciousness slipping away. The effects of the adrenaline begin to abate and your brain starts registering the searing pain delivered by millions of nociceptors in the tissues and organs of your body. The last thing you remember is a flurry of gnats and no-see-ums flitting over your face, attracted by the blood spilling onto the trail.

In another hour or so, a troop of boy scouts will come marching around the large boulder, chanting songs, clapping hands, and doing everything else their scouting handbook recommends to ward off bears. Your corpse will serve as a not-so-gentle reminder that they can never be too safe.

swim with the fishes

The man commented that it had been an enjoyable swim—
until he looked down and noticed that one of his nipples
was missing.

—*TORONTO STAR*, 1994, DESCRIBING A SWIMMER ATTACKED
BY PIRANHAS

For your fortieth birthday you wanted some real adventure. The
Website for Extreme Amazon Encounters looked perfect: it promised
you a week's worth of rustic camping, hikes through the rainforest,
and exotic fishing trips. What it *didn't* promise was a lazy, inattentive
guide and a gaggle of elderly, overweight traveling companions—but
these are the people you appear to be stuck with. By 8:30 A.M. on
day four of the trip, your gear is packed and you've finished breakfast—but everyone else at your campsite is still fast asleep. You're

determined to get the most out of your vacation, so you embark on a little solo sight-seeing.

You drag one of the canoes into the water, hop aboard, and paddle some five hundred yards down the river. The mighty Amazon is dense with wildlife—in the tree branches overhead, you observe brilliant green kingfishers and magnificent blue macaws. You even glimpse a rare uakari monkey on the bank of the river, peering at you through some shrubbery. You paddle closer to get a better look, but your canoe grinds to a halt against the sandy river bottom. Startled by your approach, the monkey scampers into the woods. You find your-self resting on a very large sandbar.

You strip off your shoes and socks, roll up your khakis, and step out of your canoe. The shallow water is very murky and you can't see where you're walking. You have no idea that during the months of June through December—known along the Amazon as the "dry season"—schools of piranha will find themselves moored in the shallow sections of the river. Cut off from an adequate food supply, these piranhas have little to eat except occasional fruits and berries that drop into the river. By the time your meaty calves begin wading along shore, the red-bellied piranhas waiting there are mighty hungry.

These are no ordinary fish. Although piranhas aren't much larger than a good-sized goldfish, they have the dentition to clear the flesh off any animal's bones—including yours. A piranha can go from open mouth to clenched teeth in less than five milliseconds—that's less time than it takes you to blink. Their jaws have an interlocking design: the top triangular teeth fit snugly into the gaps between the bottom teeth, snapping shut like a steel trap. And each individual tooth is as sharp as a razor blade.

Piranhas also have excellent senses: good vision, a well-developed sense of smell, and a system of pores along their body that allows them to detect distant disturbances in the water. When your splashing feet enter their territory, the nearest piranha is thirty yards away—but it can cover that distance in a few seconds. As you wrestle with your canoe, pushing and pulling it over the sandbank, you suddenly feel an unspeakable pain and yank your left foot out of the water. It is a curious sight: where you once had five toes, there are now only four. Your big toe is missing, and blood is spurting everywhere.

There are plenty of nerves in this relatively small piece of your anatomy. The joint of the toe features a large medial digital nerve. The soft tissue is rich with peripheral nerves, and the *periosteum* (a lining that encases the bone of your big toe) has even more nerves that specifically communicate bone trauma. When cut, all of these nerves absorb chemicals that are carried back to the spine and signal exaggerated sensitivity to the brain. The end result is a lot of pain— it feels like a red-hot poker is being pressed against the wound.

You're so startled that you nearly lose your balance and plant your foot back in the water. As you do this, the piranha who claimed your toe is signaling to his friends with a sonic communication system (it's the piranha's equivalent of a dinner bell). In the time it takes you to realize that you should probably get the hell out of the water, another two hundred fish have joined the party. A school of piranha can inflict about twelve hundred bites per minute (or twenty bites per second). In an instant, there are large chunks missing from both of your legs.

The pain literally knocks you off your feet. You land face first in the shallow water, putting more of your flesh into the feeding zone. You push yourself up with your hands and shout for help, but realize you're on your own. Even if your geriatric traveling companions could hear you, there's no way they could paddle down the river in time to help. Your brain signals your autonomic nervous system and the physical symptoms of panic set in. Your breathing accelerates and your heart races. The hungry piranhas wriggle up the legs of your pants, seeking out every surface of available flesh.

Each bite feels like a knife wound—like your body is being stabbed in a hundred different places at once. Countless nerve receptors are transmitting signals from so many different places that your brain stops distinguishing which hurt is coming from where. The frenzied thrashing of the piranhas makes the water surface appear like a pool of boiling blood.

The one nice thing about death by piranha is that the sudden loss of blood quickly renders you unconscious. As you bleed to death from hundreds of lacerations, your bones are picked clean by the thrashing mob of fish. They eat everything—flesh, muscles, and organs—and you are reduced to a pile of bones and a pair of shredded khakis. It's no wonder Extreme Amazon Encounters made you sign that insurance waiver . . .

jellyfish jamboree

jellyfish jamboreeoree

On some beaches, the season is shaping up like some kind of science-fiction movie. I've never seen anything like it.

—DEREK SHOCKRO, A LIFEGUARD ON REHOBOTH BEACH, DELAWARE, 1999

It's one of those hot, sticky days at the Jersey shore, and you've been keeping cool with a long ocean swim. Your girlfriend is back on shore, working on her tan, and after an hour in the water, you decide to join her.

As you wade through the waist-deep water, you can't help but notice the four cute girls in bikinis who are flirting with the lifeguard; you're completely unaware that an object resembling a brown plastic bag is slowly drifting in your direction. You see it at the last moment and quickly jump back. Although you've managed to avoid contact, you suddenly feel an intense stinging pain across both of your legs. You don't know what's happening but understand that you must get back to shore—fast. Only your legs are quickly becoming numb and you're not sure if you can make it.

While swimming in the idyllic seaside village of Deal, New Jersey, you haven't encountered anything more horrifying than a used prophylactic—but dangerous jellyfish lurk in nearly every body of saltwater on the planet, and you've just been kissed by one. These sea creatures have been around for almost 650 million years (longer than dinosaurs, in fact), and there are more than six hundred different species. These curios of marine life are ninety-five percent water, have no head or brain, no eyes or ears, no heart, lungs, or gills, no bones, and no blood—but they all sting in order to capture their prey. Fortunately, only a few dozen of the hundreds of species of jellyfish are harmful to humans.

The nastiest of them is known as the box jelly—the world's most venomous sea creature. Venom from the box jelly will stop the heart of an adult in as little as three minutes. In Australia, box jellies have killed even more swimmers than sharks.

Thankfully, you live in New Jersey, where the Atlantic Ocean is free of box jellies, but home to the occasional lion's mane. Like all jellyfish, the lion's mane doesn't hunt its prey—it just drifts in the water, stunning small fish, crustaceans, and plankton, and then eats them. The sting of a lion's mane will hurt like hell but—barring an extreme allergic reaction—will not kill you. It is simply a niftily constructed natural annoyance.

A lion's mane has a reddish body that is six to eight inches wide; it's shaped like a bell made of two layers of tissue, known as the epidermis and gastrodermis. A hole in the gastrodermis serves as both its mouth and waste hole. It has no internal organs other than a simple stomach and reproductive organ. Trailing the body are long tentacles covered with thousands of stinging cells called *cnidocytes*.

That brown bag you saw floating in the water was actually the jellyfish's body (or "bell"); its tentacles, hidden below the surface of the water, made contact with your legs and set off a painful chain of events. Its stinging cells are covered with harpoon-like structures called *nematocysts*—they begin like pushed-in fingers on a glove, then evert and fire.

Hundreds of tiny sharp hooks puncture the epidermis layer of your skin, and the jellyfish emits a toxin made of a number of different proteins.

This toxin interferes with your nerve synapses and causes numbness in your legs. An enzyme in the toxin results in a steady and searing pain. As you start to scream and flail in the water, many swimmers in your vicinity have their own scare—they figure you're being attacked by a shark, and quickly run for shore. Up and down the beach, you've incited a wave of panic. Kids are shouting "Shark! Shark!" and pointing in your direction.

You crawl to shore and instinctively grab your legs, but that only makes them hurt more. They're covered with a number of red lesions, and attached to these lesions are strange white bits that look like tissue paper. These white bits are actually pieces of the jellyfish that adhered to your skin; by touching them, you only cause more of the nematocysts to fire. (Jellyfish tentacles remain venomous for up to six months—even on dry land.)

Spectators circle around you, offering various suggestions, when suddenly the lifeguard comes bounding over the sand. "You're going to be okay," he assures you. "It's just a jelly." He's carrying a jellyfish sting kit that contains, of all things, vinegar and shaving cream. The lifeguard pours the vinegar on your legs, which inactivates the cells that have yet to fire, providing a bit of relief. He then applies shaving cream to your leg and scrapes away the remaining nematocysts with a credit card.

"You here with anyone?" the lifeguard asks.

"My girlfriend," you tell him, "but I don't want her to see me like this." Too late: She's already witnessed the commotion and is watching your rescue from a safe distance. You can't really be sure, but it looks like she might be laughing.

Half an hour later, at the hospital, you receive a topical steroid cream to heal the rashes and an antihistamine that slows your reaction to the toxin. Your relationship, however, will not heal. It turns out that, while you were frolicking in the ocean, your girl struck up a conversation with some bodybuilder who's not, in her words, "afraid of a stupid little jellyfish."

pamplonaaah!ah!

I put my hand back there and I could feel a big hole in my back. I stuck my thumb in my back. I could feel the blood just going . . .

—JOHN TORPEY, GORED IN PAMPLONA, SPAIN, 1994

You're approaching a sharp turn in one of Pamplona's most narrow streets when you hear a thundering noise that is clearly not the pounding of human feet. You follow the turn of the curve, running alongside a wooden barricade that lines the road. The sound of the stampede grows louder. Suddenly you lose your footing, trip, and stumble to the wet cobblestone, landing face first. Your nose hits the ground the hardest and you taste blood in your mouth. You try to stand up by pushing your hands to the street and raising your hind quarters in the air—unwittingly creating the perfect target for a bull that's directly behind you, charging with its six-inch horns aimed at your posterior.

Around the world, the annual running of the bulls in Pamplona, Spain, is perceived as an exotic cultural event. (Thanks in large part to its romantic portrayal in Ernest Hemingway's 1926 novel *The Sun Also Rises*.) But the locals understand the inherent danger of this activity—a centerpiece to the annual Fiesta de San Fermín—and affectionately refer to it as "the three-minute death game."

On eight consecutive mornings in July, six adult bulls, weighing up to 1,400 pounds each and specially bred to attack, will stampede to the bullring along a half-mile of narrow cobblestone streets. Just ahead of them will be more than a thousand daredevil runners—a mix of locals and *turistas* from around the world. Two hundred medical personnel are on standby to tend to the inevitable carnage; since 1923, thirteen participants have been killed (most recently an American in 1995). But these statistics don't stop the six-hundred-year-old ritual and they certainly won't stop you. *Olé!*

The daredevils begin to congregate at dawn—right after the bars close—and you're among the throng that gathers on Santo Domingo, where the race begins. To stay sharp, you abstained from drinking the night before—but now you're so anxious, you wish you'd taken a few shots to calm your nerves. The body responds to your fear by triggering faster breathing, a widening of your pupils, an increased blood flow, and a flood of adrenaline. Your heart is pounding.

As the magic moment approaches, the boisterous crowd becomes eerily quiet. Then, at exactly eight o'clock, a small rocket bursts into the blue sky—and everyone starts to run. You find it difficult to move in such a large group of people, but you fight your way through the throng, stepping on the heels of the runner in front of you. Your focus is on nothing but moving forward. Perspiration trickles down your forehead and stings your eyes.

Twenty seconds later, a second rocket fires. You shudder slightly, knowing this means the bulls have been released. You don't have nearly as much of a head start as you'd like. The pace of the runners quickens and you work harder to keep up. Your heartbeat accelerates to fuel the extra stress placed on your muscles. Longtime veterans of the festival say that the first two hundred meters are its most dangerous stretch, because the bulls are full of energy and confused by the noise of the crowd. You know that if you can last a few more minutes, most of the danger will be far behind you.

The street begins to slope upward, and as everyone's pace slows, you're certain you can hear the clattering hooves. Spectators all around you are cheering from their balconies, or from behind the protection of wooden barricades. But when they start pointing and shouting, you're certain the bulls are getting close. These animals don't necessarily want to hassle with you—but if you get in their way, they're not going to alter their course. (In fact, there's a small group of men running behind them, beating the bulls with sticks and encouraging them to hurry along.)

In your mad dash to stay ahead of the bulls, you don't notice that you've crossed onto a slick patch of wet cobblestone—until it's too late. You fall forward just as the first of the bulls is charging right behind you. Its horns are taped for your protection, but they smash so hard into your buttocks that the dull tips still pierce your skin, tissue, and gluteus maximus muscle. The force of the hit lifts you into the air and throws you aside as the bull continues its run. You feel more shock than pain, but you struggle to get up, knowing that the remaining five bulls must be closing in fast. And you're right— before you even get to your knees, you're being pummeled by another 1,200 pounds of force.

That's the second time you've made the mistake of getting up—a better strategy would be staying down with your hands clasped over your head. You can't help but wonder if you're still in one piece— and then another of the massive animals comes stampeding over your body. A woman on a balcony begins shouting for a *médico*.

You try crawling toward the wooden barricade, but you cannot move. One of the bull's hooves has shattered a vertebra in the top of your back, severing all communication between your brain and your limbs. Another hoof has fractured your skull, causing a tear in the middle meningeal artery that supplies blood to the lining of your brain. This blood quickly leaks into your brain cavity and literally drowns part of the organ. Within moments, your vision of the crowded street begins to fade, and you lose consciousness. The *médicos* come swiftly to your aid, but the hemorrhage in your brain is too fast to be controlled.

The romance is dead—and so are you.

PART II

THE GREAT
OUTDOORS

hot and bothered

In between periods of feverish babble, I pondered my predicament. My life depended on being able to walk and I couldn't even stand.

—AUTHOR GRAHAM MACKINTOSH, WHO SPENT 500 DAYS IN THE DESERT OF BAJA CALIFORNIA, 1988

You've always been a sucker for long shots, and a city like Las Vegas offers plenty of 'em: a spin of the roulette wheel, a roll of the dice, a shuffle of cards, or a pull on the slot machines—you'll bet on just about anything. You'll also borrow to stay in the game, and now a recent losing streak has landed you in a heap of trouble with your creditors. Someone must have guessed that you were planning to skip town, because in the middle of the night three beefy guys came crashing into your hotel room—and now you're blindfolded, bound, gagged, and tumbling around inside the trunk of a Plymouth Valiant.

The car travels for about two hours without stopping, and then suddenly the driver slams on the brakes. Two strong arms hoist you out of the trunk and throw you to the ground. You receive three sharp kicks to the kidneys that knock the wind out of you, and then someone unties your wrists. By the time you pull off your blindfold, the Valiant is peeling toward the dusty horizon, where the sun is just beginning to surface. Surrounding you in every direction is the kind of landscape that you've only seen in movies—a dry, featureless desert stretching as far as the eye can see. You're willing to bet that the Valiant is driving in the direction of the nearest town, so you dust yourself off and begin following the tire tracks on foot.

Get ready for a long walk. A desert is classified as any land that receives less than ten inches of precipitation a year. Our planet features forty-nine million square kilometers of desert (that's twenty-nine times the size of Alaska) and the arid landscape supports only specialized life forms that have adapted to withstand the harshest of conditions. People are not one of those life forms. Under extreme heat and without basic necessities, chief among them water, human beings are always at risk.

People often underestimate the debilitating nature of extreme heat, which can transform a simple day hike or unexpected flat tire into a life-or-death situation. Experts recommend that anyone driving through a desert should pack at least three gallons of fresh drinking water for each person in the vehicle—not to mention waterproof matches, a knife, first aid kit, and metal signaling mirror. Even in well-traveled areas like Arizona's Grand Canyon, park rangers perform more than four hundred search-and-rescue operations a year.

In addition to snakes, scorpions, and unforgiving mobsters, the biggest dangers in the desert are heatstroke and dehydration. In a more temperate environment, a human being could survive about three days without water, but in desert terrain even a single day can be fatal. Heatstroke occurs when the body cannot cool itself due to the extreme temperatures and dehydration. Not unlike a car, a person simply overheats and dies. With adequate supplies and proper training, it's possible to beat the desert at its own game. But for someone like you—accustomed to the air-conditioned climates of the casinos and all-you-can-eat clam strip buffets—the day will be merciless.

It begins easily enough—at dawn, the sun hangs low in the sky, and the sand is still cool beneath your feet. Your creditors have relieved you of all your clothes except a tank top, boxer shorts, and socks, so you're walking freely at a brisk pace. But the long drive into the desert has left you feeling thirsty, and after an hour of hard walking, you're already fantasizing about those complimentary water bottles that you usually get at the craps table.

By ten o'clock, the sun is blindingly bright, and its ultraviolet rays start burning cells on the surface of your skin. Your body absorbs heat in three ways: directly from the sun's rays, from the hot air, and from the heat reflected off the ground. You wrap your tank top around your head in an effort to protect your face, which is getting the worst of the burn—but this just exposes more of your back and chest. You plow ahead, glancing occasionally at the horizon, hoping to glimpse vegetation or a rocky outcropping, or anything that could produce a little shade. The temperature is well past one hundred degrees and the heat is sapping your energy; your mouth, tongue, and throat are absolutely parched.

Meanwhile, the interior of your body is doing its best to keep up. The dermis layer of your skin is producing sweat and expelling it through tiny pores. This moisture on the surface of your body is generated to remove excess heat and cool you. Unfortunately, this process also increases your dehydration, since it's flushing excess moisture through the skin. You're not aware that it's happening, but the simple actions of sweating and breathing are expelling a considerable percentage of your body's water weight.

The average adult human is made up of approximately sixty percent water and it's vital to just about every function, from blood flow to muscle contraction. At 165 pounds, your body includes about fifty quarts of water. You lose about three quarts per day through normal activity, but this supply is usually replenished by the water in juices, soda, and other beverages (now you know why so many doctors advise you to supplement your daily intake with eight 8-ounce glasses of water). Losing two quarts without replenishment will lead to the onset of dehydration symptoms; losing seven quarts or more could be fatal.

Just before two o'clock, you take your first break and collapse in the red dust underneath your feet. You'd wager the temperature is somewhere around 120 degrees, and the ground feels hot enough to fry an egg (that's no exaggeration—with the kind of climate you're in, the ground will literally bake to nearly 180 degrees). You rest just long enough to catch your breath, then stand up and press on. At this point, you know that stopping for the night will result in death. It's much better to keep walking, until the sunset will bring a bit of relief from the extreme temperature.

But the day seems endless. As you walk farther, you are surprised to find that you are sweating much less. Your skin becomes almost dry as your body purges most of its excess water content. Now the water in your individual cells is drying up, and consequently these cells are beginning to malfunction and die. Along with the moisture, essential body salts such as sodium, potassium, calcium bicarbonate, and phosphate are being expelled with the fluids. This electrolyte imbalance causes terrible cramping in your arms, legs, and stomach.

After eight hours in the sun, you've lost about five quarts of water and are ten percent dehydrated—the point at which most people will suffer from deadly heatstroke. You have to close your eyes to keep the featureless landscape from spinning. You can't come up with a plan—you're not even sure where you are. It's difficult to breathe and you kneel down for just a moment, then collapse face forward into the sand, unconscious.

Even as a long shot, your odds of living much longer are not terribly good . . .

ice, ice baby

My toes felt like frozen blocks.

**—A CLIMBER FROM COLORADO IN DENALI NATIONAL PARK,
ALASKA, 2000**

After the first three hours of strenuous walking, you realize you should have gone with a size eleven. Just a week earlier, you were safe and sound in the climate-controlled temperature of your local shopping mall, browsing a selection of hiking boots; your feet felt good and snug in a size ten, but the salesman suggested that you go with a size eleven. Since he was just a teenager, probably earning minimum wage, you decided to trust your own instincts—and now you're going to pay for it.

When you purchased your boots, you didn't anticipate that you'd be wearing three pairs of very thick wool socks, and now your feet are killing you. At first you hoped the boots just needed to be broken in, but now you understand that they simply don't fit. To make matters worse, you have this realization when you're about three hours from your car, hiking through the White Mountains of New Hampshire at an altitude of about 5,000 feet. The frigid December wind has picked up considerably, blowing arctic-cold air across your face. Your destination is a lodge at the top of the mountain but you consider turning back—there's no way you want to travel another hour in these boots, let alone a full weekend. When you come upon a small mountain lake, you stop for a moment to catch your breath and contemplate your next move.

You don't realize it, but you're standing on some freshly frozen water near the lake's edge. It suddenly cracks, and your entire left boot is immersed in thirty-degree water. A moment later, you're scrambling backward, but the damage is already done: the icy water has spilled through the top of your boot, soaking your wool socks and leaving your foot encased in a wet, squishy mess.

When meat's placed in a freezer, it freezes. If you're stuck outside in freezing temperatures, your body will do the same. Since the body will automatically conserve blood and heat for your major internal organs, it's your extremities that are most vulnerable to frostbite—your nose, ears, fingers, and toes.

There are different degrees of frostbite, but at its worst, the skin, tissue, and bone will freeze and die. You don't have to be on the summit of Mount Everest, either—if you're exposed to freezing temperatures, consider yourself at risk. Frostbite can and does happen to people accidentally locked out of their houses, or even commuters just cleaning ice off their car windshields. In 1996, a salesman in northern Wisconsin stopped for a few drinks before returning to the mobile home that served as his sales office. Once he reached the trailer, the door proved to be too complicated for him to operate, and he passed out while trying to enter. The next morning, a doctor had to amputate all of his fingers.

When you embarked on your hike to the lodge, the notion of frostbite never even crossed your mind. Sure, it's cold outside—when you began the walk, the temperature was hovering in the high teens. But you're properly dressed in an expensive parka, several layers of warm clothing, a hat, a neckwarmer, gloves, and those three pairs of socks. Unfortunately, none of these items can help the fact that your boot is full of water.

You begin heading back to your car. Already, the blood vessels near the surface of your foot are beginning to constrict, and this causes a tingling pain because blood cannot flow at its usual pace. There's also eighteen inches of snow on the ground, so your foot doesn't get a moment's respite from the freezing temperatures. As the wet socks rub against your skin, they remove natural oils that help to protect the body from frostbite; they also conduct heat away from your foot. The wind around you is kicking up, and it feels like the temperature has dropped to five below.

You realize you need to dry your foot—quickly—so you sit down and remove your boot and your socks. This is a very big mistake: exposing your wet foot to subzero temperatures only makes it colder. You see that the skin looks very white, almost bloodless; to conserve heat, your blood is steering clear of the foot's surface tissue, which consequently begins to freeze. At the same time, this tissue is also dehydrating because water is exiting its cells through the process of osmosis. The water has nowhere to go except into the bloodstream, where it thickens the blood. And thicker blood has an even harder time passing through constricted vessels, so the flow to your foot is gradually diverted.

You tie your scarf around your foot in an attempt to make a crude sock, and then stuff your foot back in the boot and resume your climb down the mountain. Unfortunately, your car is still a few hours away—and the temperature is still dropping. As you hurry down the mountain, trying to move as quickly as possible, the remaining water in the tissue of your toes is freezing. The resulting ice crystals will inevitably damage the blood vessels, perhaps permanently.

The one good thing about your situation is that frostbite has destroyed most of the nerves in your foot, so you don't feel very much pain. In fact, you don't feel much of anything. (In many cases, this lack of painful sensation will delay a frostbite diagnosis for hours, which increases your risk for damage.) You feel like you're walking on an icy stump; your toes are dead weight, and you fear that the damage may be irreversible. You're panicked, and you begin to dread the very real possibility of hypothermia—a severe decrease in body temperature that can be deadly.

But you make it to your car, and with directions from the closest gas station attendant, you begin driving to the nearest hospital, which is nearly an hour away. Fortunately, you don't think to warm your toes in front of your car's heater—excessive warming can cause even more damage to the tissue. The same is true for trying to rub life back into the damaged area.

When you do arrive at a hospital, your toes are badly blistered. The prescribed treatment is immediate immersion in a temperature-controlled water bath of one hundred degrees; as the tissue thaws, the damaged nerves become active again, and the resulting pain is an intense tingling sensation. The doctors respond to your suffering by giving you intravenous morphine, and soon you're feeling much more comfortable.

But you're far from being out of the woods. After a few days, dark blood blisters cover your feet, signaling the death of skin and possibly deeper tissue. Unfortunately, until the tissue has had a chance to fully recover (usually about six weeks), there's no way to tell how much deep tissue is dead, or if the damage is irreversible. In the meantime, your toes are horrifically painful to the touch, and you can't put any weight on your foot. It's little consolation to think that if your toes must be amputated, those size-ten hiking boots will fit you perfectly.

say it ain't snow

I heard a deep, muffled thunk. Then it was like someone pulled the rug out from under me and I instantly flopped down onto the snow, losing all the speed I had built up.

—BRUCE TREMPER, DIRECTOR OF THE UTAH AVALANCHE FORECAST
CENTER, 1978

It comes without warning. One moment, you're enjoying a great run on undisturbed white powder, zigzagging through the backwoods of the Colorado Rocky Mountains. The next moment, the snow has swept you up like a tidal wave, and you're being whipped around like an old sock in a washing machine. Your poles are yanked away; one of your skis flies over your shoulder. You can't see where you're going—you can barely breathe—and at any moment, you expect to collide with a tree, break your neck, and die.

Snowflakes conjure such tranquil images. Light and ephemeral, they float through the air before settling to the ground in a peaceful white blanket. But this "blanket" can move without warning and deliver a force of up to 20,000 pounds of pressure per square foot—enough to level a concrete building. When this happens, you're dealing with an avalanche, one of nature's most awesome killers, and your chances of survival are slim. If you're near a lot of snow on an incline, the risk is always present—in fact, it's literally right under your feet.

Avalanches kill about two hundred people around the world each year, and the victims are largely recreationists. France, Austria, and Switzerland have more avalanches than any other part of the world—but if you're looking to find one in the United States, Colorado is the place to be, especially during the months of January, February, and March, when snowfall amounts are at their peak.

To understand why avalanches happen, it helps to understand the transformation of snow as it falls from the sky and settles to the earth. When new flakes form in the atmosphere, their structure is shaped like a crystal, which gives them a feathery appearance and allows them to bond easily with other flakes. In most places, the first snowfall of winter is perfectly harmless and could not cause an avalanche by itself. But a subsequent snowfall serves to insulate this bottom layer, trapping warm water vapor. (This is particularly true in early winter, when the ground temperature is still warmer than the air temperature.)

This trapped water vapor will evaporate upward and freeze onto the edges of the newer, colder snow. The result is a layer of snowflakes with smooth edges that do not bond with other snow. Known as *depth hoar*, this layer will remain trapped under new snow as tremendous weight and pressure builds due to subsequent snowfalls, until the slightest provocation causes the layers to move. The resultant shift of snow can be catastrophic.

Of course, you're not the type of person who worries about such things. You ski double black diamonds for warm-ups and love exploring the Rocky Mountain backcountry, miles away from the crowded man-made slopes that tourists flock to. You've always held a disdain for megalodges with their super-high-speed lifts and expensive cappuccino bars. You're even more disdainful of the clientele—all those yuppies in their L.L. Bean jackets and gloves stuffed with disposable hand warmers, carrying overpriced compasses and other expensive, unnecessary survival gear.

As you're zigzagging across the powder, you feel lighter than air—but you're actually just enough force to separate the upper and lower layers of snow that are divided by the delicate depth hoar. From underneath your skis, you hear a sudden "whoompf" sound, as the top slab of snow is dislodged and begins to move. You look down at your feet and can't believe what you see: even though you're hurtling down the mountain, the snow underneath your skis appears to be sliding *ahead* of you.

In trepidation, you look back, and the entire mountain looks like it's collapsing. Terrified, you bend your knees and lean forward, trying to ski even faster but knowing that you can't outrace several thousand square feet of snow. When you're finally hit from behind, it feels like someone has thrown a sandbag at your neck; you fall forward and begin to tumble.

You try paddling your arms to essentially "swim" to the surface of this maelstrom. But the snow is exerting too much force in too many different directions—you just end up flailing. As your muscles increase their demand for oxygen, you begin gasping for air, but every time you open your mouth, it fills with snow. It's ironic, but as a victim of an avalanche, one of the biggest threats to your life right now is "drowning." Given that avalanches can easily approach speeds of fifty miles per hour, you also have good reason to worry about colliding with a tree, a rock, or another natural barrier.

The snow tosses you over and underneath its surface; every glimpse of daylight is followed by a fall into darkness. As your body struggles for oxygen, you become more and more confused—but just when you feel like you're about to pass out, the snow slows to a stop. You are now completely buried, and it's pitch black.

When wet snow moves, the air between individual crystals is quickly squeezed out. As a result, the snow around your body quickly hardens like poured cement. You can't move a muscle. You don't know what kind of injuries you might have—broken bones, cuts, even paralysis. The ski goggles dangling around your mouth have created a tiny reservoir of oxygen, but it's not going to last long. As you exhale warm carbon dioxide, the snow around you melts and refreezes, creating an icy shell that blocks the flow of fresh air from the surface.

Every instinct is telling you to simply get up, but you're not even sure which way up is. You spit some snow out of your mouth and notice that the saliva dribbles back onto your face—which suggests that you must be lying on your back. But you're still encased in packed snow that is quickly lowering your body temperature.

This is a dangerous situation: If your body temperature drops just 1.5 degrees below the normal 98.6, your brain will start to fail, affecting simple judgment and later, consciousness. On top of this, the oxygen in your frozen sarcophagus is nearly depleted, and you feel like you could just go to sleep forever as the initial stages of *hypoxia*—or oxygen deprivation—begin to affect your brain.

But today is your lucky day. When the avalanche started, a tourist snowshoeing on a parallel trail witnessed the entire event. He quickly raced to the area where he last saw you, and noticed that your ski tip is protruding from the surface. It's your good fortune that this man has chosen to invest in some overpriced survival gear from L.L. Bean—specifically, a small collapsible shovel that he keeps in his backpack.

With the help of this tool, the man digs as hard and fast as he can, knowing that time is of the essence. The probability of survival for a person extricated within fifteen minutes is ninety-two percent—but after thirty-five minutes, that rate drops to a mere thirty percent.

Underneath the snow, you are closing your eyes. You realize this snowy grave will be your final resting place, but you're simply too weak to panic. Then you hear a faint voice shouting that help is on the way. Are you imagining it? Suddenly, an arm bursts through the snow and sunlight shines on your face. You've never been so happy to see a fellow outdoorsman in your life. This person shovels you out of the snow and assesses your condition; remarkably, you appear to have no broken bones and no major injuries. It looks like you're going to make it.

And next year? Maybe you'll invest in some overpriced survival gear for yourself.

drown and out

There wasn't anything I could do. I thought I was going
to die.

—JEREMY JOHNS, SURVIVOR OF A NEAR-DROWNING IN LAKE
WASHINGTON, 1999

In the moments before your demise, you're reminded of a game that
you played as a child: You and your brother would sit at the bottom of
a swimming pool, competing to see who could hold his breath the
longest. After a minute or so, the game would start to hurt; you'd feel
a burn in your chest and the oxygen deprivation would leave you
light-headed. Eventually, your body's survival instincts would overcome
your willpower to win a stupid game, and you would come flailing to
the surface, gasping for breath.

Your current situation is quite similar, but this time it's no game. For reasons you can't understand, your body's survival instincts have failed. The burning in your chest is excruciating, and you feel so light-headed you can barely think straight. All you know is that you can't open your mouth, because water will flood in and you will most likely die. But you have no choice.

About 4,000 Americans drown each year. In fact, it's the tenth leading cause of death, second among people under twenty-five (behind motor vehicle accidents). Surprisingly, more than fifty percent of drownings occur in backyard pools; the ocean accounts for only ten percent of drowning accidents, thanks to the presence of lifeguards. If you're rescued and receive the proper treatment, it's possible to survive what is known as a "near-drowning" experience (being submerged and inhaling water).

Unfortunately, you're vacationing at a remote mountain lake near Saint Moritz, Switzerland, where the lifeguards are few and far between. You've spent most of the afternoon hiking around the lake's perimeter and enjoying gorgeous views of the distant Alps. Earlier that morning, one of your travel companions back at the chalet bet that if you walked long enough, you would actually see a gorgeous blonde with pigtails yodeling. But you're not getting your hopes up.

It's a warm spring day in the middle of June, and after two hours of moderate hiking you're ready for a quick dip in the still-icy waters. You're an above-average swimmer and have no qualms about heading out into the center of the lake for a cooldown. When you first jump into the water, your adrenaline carries you through the first icy plunge, and you quickly paddle toward the center of the lake, trusting that the burst of energy will warm you up. After about twenty feet, however, you realize you really just want to get out of the water—it's simply too cold to enjoy.

Even a Polar Bear would probably agree with you. The Polar Bears are a worldwide network of eccentrics who plunge into a frigid body of water just to prove their mettle—or get a free T-shirt. But in truth, the only requirement to be an official Polar Bear is to simply dip your head under the water (and then presumably make a mad dash back to an idling automobile, where the heater vents are blazing).

The water in the lake is about fifty degrees, cold enough to lower your body temperature rapidly, even more so while you're swimming. In fact, body heat loss is twenty-five percent greater in cold water than air. As soon as you hit the cold water, your body redistributes the blood flow toward the organs that need oxygen most—the heart, lungs, and brain—as a kind of survival reflex. As a result, the blood vessels in your skin and muscles will contract, making them slower, weaker, and less coordinated.

Even though you're only twenty feet from shore, you suddenly doubt if you can make it back. It's almost like your arms and legs are paralyzed, like the links between your brain and your muscles have been severed. It's a struggle just to stay afloat, and soon you're gagging on the surface of the lake. The foam in your airway initiates the vomiting reflex (just like sticking your finger down your throat), and acid from your stomach surges into your mouth, creating a nasty burning sensation.

You manage to take one last breath before slipping underneath the water; as you sink, your body temperature continues to lower, and hypothermia saps the very last of your energy. You don't know how you'll manage to resurface. Your eyes are open and, as you slowly fall, the lake appears to be growing darker. You can barely make out some underwater vegetation and a few small fish darting away from you. The Swiss sun filters down only about ten feet into the lake, and what lies beneath is a mystery.

By definition, you are already drowning. Your body is starved for oxygen and the amount of carbon monoxide in your blood is sky rocketing. In a moment you will have no choice but to breathe— your body will do it by reflex. Since you were born, a cluster of nerve cells in your brain stem has signaled your diaphragm and rib muscles to inhale. Only when you open your mouth this time, it's lake water—not oxygen—that rushes into your respiratory system. You are conscious of the odd sensation of breathing water into your lungs.

When the first drop of water enters your airway, your larynx spasms and attempts to prevent any more from passing through. But the decreased oxygen in your blood causes your larynx to relax and the floodgates to open. Fortunately, this is around the same time that you lose consciousness from the buildup of carbon dioxide in your blood.

As you sink to the bottom of the lake, the increasing water pressure forces the remaining air out of your lungs, which quickly fill with water. As a result, water (instead of oxygen) is absorbed through the lungs and into your bloodstream. This water dilutes your blood and lowers its salt concentration, which in turn upsets the body's delicate chemical and physical equilibrium, and leads to the destruction of countless red blood cells. This destruction releases large amounts of potassium, which causes your heart to beat erratically until it finally stops. When blood stops flowing to your brain, you die.

Your body slowly settles toward the bottom of the lake, head first (it's the densest part). Only hours later, when your body begins to decompose, gases produced in your tissues will make you more buoyant. As your lifeless body rises to the surface, a young woman dressed in light blue lederhosen comes skipping up the trail. Her hair is braided into pigtails and—believe it or not—she's actually yodeling. Your friend was right, but you'll never know.

blowin' in the wind

Suddenly a huge wind drew the tub and me into the air. It sent me swirling around and around, then I suddenly crashed to the ground, about thirty yards away from my house.

—BUBBA DEGRANDO, SURVIVOR OF A TEXAS TWISTER, 1998

You see it coming and you quickly slam the door. You run frantically around the house, looking for a suitable place to hunker down. Unfortunately—without a basement or storm cellar—there's no good place for you to hide. So you opt for the second best option, which is hoisting the mattress off your bed and dragging it to the bathroom. You crouch down in the tub and pull the mattress over your head. Before you're even situated, you hear the noise coming—it sounds like a train whistle but grows increasingly louder. Your entire home starts to shake. The window of your bathroom shatters and then suddenly it's like your whole world explodes.

Dorothy's fantastic trip in *The Wizard of Oz* was not pure fantasy. The tornado is one of nature's most destructive and unpredictable forces and it will lay waste to just about anything in its path—even you. But while twisters have leveled property and caused plenty of deaths, they have also (in rare cases) taken people on the thrill ride of their lives.

Three-quarters of the world's tornadoes hit the United States, and the majority will strike in Texas (with the remainder concentrated in the "tornado alley" that stretches from the Lone Star State up through the Dakotas). Scientists can't exactly explain what causes tornadoes, but they know they're created when cool, dry, dense air makes contact with warmer, moister, thinner air (like that of a thunderstorm). The dense air wants to be below the thin air, so it spirals downward like water running out of a drain; meanwhile, the warm, moist air moves upward, and the result is the tornado's vortex. In the long stretch of Tornado Alley, the warm, moist air from the Gulf of Mexico collides with cool, dry air from the Rocky Mountains, and the results can be catastrophic.

A tornado can measure anywhere from a few feet across to a mile wide, and its swirling winds can reach speeds of up to three hundred miles per hour. Between late spring and early summer of every year, some seven hundred tornadoes of varying size, intensity, and duration will strike in the United States. They cause an average of thirty deaths annually, although some of the worst individual tornadoes in history have killed hundreds at a time. And annual property damage can reach up to a billion dollars.

Through the kitchen window of your Texas trailer home, you've noticed some pretty strange weather all day long—including lots of strong winds and a fierce, pelting rain. At one point, things seem to quiet down a little, but when the winds kick up again, you swing open the door to take a look. The air smells of rock and dust, and you spy a huge swirling black cloud on the horizon.

You've never actually seen a twister before, and the sight is literally jaw-dropping. It's much wider than you ever imagined, but it moves just like the one Dorothy encountered—a swirling, spinning, funnel-shaped, black cloud. It appears to be a mile or so away and heading directly for your fiberglass and wood abode.

The fact that you live in a mobile home makes you twenty times more likely to die in a tornado. (And yet the number of mobile homes doubled between 1970 and 1990—go figure.) Experts recommend that mobile homes be tied down, but even that wouldn't do much good against the mighty power of a full-blown tornado. Given their light construction and lack of a foundation, trailer homes can be whipped up into the air and deposited miles away from their original location.

When the tornado hits, you're swept into the sky, and for the next thirty seconds the rules of gravity no longer apply to you or your home. You are tossed to and fro and feel dizzy and disoriented. It's difficult to open your eyes as sand is blowing everywhere. You are surrounded by an ear-splitting roar and barely make out shapes in the dark swirl of dirt and debris. Objects resembling your bed, television, and dresser seem to be hovering nearby; the walls of your home have been demolished, and your possessions are swirling around you like the ingredients of a chunky stew. The force of the wind is so strong it feels like your skin is being blown off your body by tiny bits of dust. You can't even open your mouth to breathe . . . or scream.

Something sharp hits your left cheek, and you feel a hot, searing sensation. In a reflex reaction you try to reach for your face, but the force of the wind keeps you from moving your limbs. A microwave oven smashes hard into your right side. Debris continues to whip around you and you brace yourself for death, praying that it will be quick and relatively painless. After about thirty seconds in hell, you begin to fall downward, and you are quickly separated from the vortex and the scattered remains of your house. You land hard on your back.

You open your eyes but you can't see; they've been caked over with mud and sand. When you manage to wipe away some of the dirt, you detect the familiar red and white logo of a Kentucky Fried Chicken restaurant. This seems slightly strange to you, because you live at least two miles away from the closest KFC. Scattered across the drive-through lane are many of your belongings, including your computer, one of your stereo speakers, and an assortment of your clothes. The KFC is unharmed, and a handful of patrons are staring at you through the window, like you're an alien that has dropped out of the sky.

As the excitement winds down, the pain kicks in. Your left cheek feels like it's been ripped off—but in reality, your television antennae twisted like a corkscrew and embedded itself in the soft tissue of your face. The rest of your body is vaguely throbbing—especially your right arm, which is badly broken. Your collision with the microwave oven was so forceful that it appears to have cracked your ulna, the larger of the two bones in your forearm. As the broken bone presses into the muscle and tissue, the surrounding nerve endings send a very clear message to your brain. The dermis layer of your skin chimes in with its own messages of pain; you've just been pelted by hundreds of small household objects, rocks, and debris, and these bruises will take a long time to heal.

But they will heal, and it's a miracle you're alive. Through the window of the KFC restaurant, you can see the manager on the telephone, gesturing wildly as he describes your arrival to the 911 operator. Knowing that help is on the way, you close your eyes and relax. If there's any money from an insurance company, you're going to put it toward buying a sturdier house. Or maybe you'll ask that manager about investing in a nice, durable KFC franchise.

sinking in quicksand

By the second day I started worrying. Doggone, there's nobody down here, and there might not be anyone coming, I dug all around me with that stick, digging quickly, trying to get my feet free. I was so physically tired. I could hardly do a thing.

—BOB SEBOR, STUCK IN QUICKSAND, COYLE, OKLAHOMA, 2000

The first few steps feel just like mud. You sink to the tops of your sneakers, and the only thing you're worried about is ruining a pair of Reeboks. But since the damage is already done, you press on. Now you're up to your ankles in the thick muck, and with your next step, you suddenly begin to sink. The once-solid ground is absorbing you like water, and before you can even react, you've been swallowed up to your waist by quicksand.

It may sound like something from an old *Gilligan's Island* episode, but quicksand is very real, and it's not restricted to uncharted tropical islands. In fact, it can be found anywhere there's water and sand in close proximity—like a creek bed, the shoreline, or even in dry back-country where there are hidden underground springs.

Quicksand forms when the water runs underneath a mixture of sand and mud. This water separates the individual grains of sand, which eliminates contact and friction, and reduces the sand's overall strength. As a result, the sand begins to take on many characteristics of a liquid—but to the untrained eye, it still looks very much like a solid.

Fortunately, most beds of quicksand are only a few inches to a few feet deep. In a typical encounter, you'll sink at most up to your knees—and if you carefully retrace your steps, you'll walk away from the experience a little dirtier and a little wiser. It's also impossible to "drown" in quicksand, per se, because your body's density is lower than that of the quicksand (which means you'll generally float). But if you panic, it's very easy to slip deeper into the muck, and just one mouthful of the thick dirt could lead to asphyxiation.

When encountering quicksand, experienced hikers will lift their legs and try to get on their backs (this evenly distributes the body's density). They'll also travel through quicksand country with a good-sized stick or pole; as soon as they start to sink, they'll rest the pole on the surface of the quicksand, then ease themselves on top of it and slowly shimmy their way back to solid ground.

But you don't travel with a pole. Heck, you don't even travel with a compass. You live in northern California, and you're the kind of person who goes day-hiking in sneakers, a baseball cap, and a T-shirt advertising your favorite defunct dotcom. For the last hour or so, you've been walking along an overgrown trail that runs parallel to a creek. The trail never comes very close to the water and you've always assumed that you're walking on dry land. But ground water (fed by the creek) has created an upward flow that extends to the surface of the trail. The result is a bed of quicksand that's almost six feet deep.

You try kicking your legs, attempting to propel yourself out of the goo. But as you move, your displaced body mass creates a vacuum that sucks you down; the more you move your body, the faster you sink. The viscous sand quickly rises up to your chest and shoulders, hugging your body like freshly poured cement. You raise your arms and beat them against the dirt, but it's no use. You are now buried almost to your neck, but you finally realize that, if you keep still, you will not sink.

So now what? The overgrown trail looks like no one has used it in months, and you haven't told any friends about your destination. You realize that, without some aid, you could remain trapped in the quicksand for hours, even days.

You try screaming for help: "Is anybody out there? Can anybody hear me?" You try clawing at the wet sand, to "pull" yourself to the surface, but it just slips through your fingers. You even try "swimming" to solid ground by using the breaststroke; after fifteen minutes, you're completely exhausted, and you appear to have moved about a quarter-inch.

The hot sun beats down on your face and your lips are dry and cracked. You start to feel very thirsty. You're also beginning to wonder why you ever went hiking in the first place. With all of California's movie multiplexes and shopping malls, whatever possessed you to take a walk in the woods? Why couldn't you have just stayed home and surfed the Web?

A half an hour later, when a hiker comes bounding down the trail, you're certain you're hallucinating—until he takes one look at your disembodied head, floating in the middle of the trail, and jumps back in terror. "Hey, are you all right?" he asks.

"I'm fine," you tell him, "just get me out of here."

You notice that he's walking with a stout wooden branch. "You're going to be okay," he says. "Just grab on and I'll pull you out." It's not quite so easy, of course—when he pulls on the branch, you only budge a few inches. But it's progress nevertheless, and you're grateful for it. The hiker explains that his name is Chris, and he says he never hikes through quicksand country without carrying an escape pole.

"I'll remember that for next time," you tell him, even though you have no intention of entering another forest—or even walking on grass—for the rest of your life. It takes a lot of heaving, grunting, and pulling to get you out of the quicksand, and when you finally emerge, you are covered in mud. But aside from a little sunburn on your face, you're going to be all right.

You follow Chris down the trail, heading back toward your car, but after a few feet you realize your beloved Oakland A's cap is missing. You thank Chris again and tell him you're going back for your hat. When you return to the bed of quicksand, you see your hat is floating on the opposite side. You don't want to get too close, so you step off the trail and start trampling through the foliage, taking the long way around.

But then, all at once, you're up to your knees in the earth again—and there's a familiar sinking feeling. "Chris!" you shout. "Come back!"

bomb voyage!

My first impression of the explosion was the very intense flash of light, and a sensation of heat on the parts of my body that were exposed. Although I did not look directly towards the object, I had the impression that suddenly the countryside became brighter than in full daylight.

—ENRICO FERMI, AN OBSERVER OF THE FIRST ATOMIC EXPLOSION,
NEW MEXICO, 1945

In the moments before sunrise, the New Mexico desert is cool and quiet, just the way you like it. You've been living here for nearly five months now. After your wife moved out, your dog died, and you lost your job at the auto plant, there was no reason to stay home anymore. You've always been fond of the outdoors—specifically the desert—so you packed your most valuable belongings into a knapsack and headed into the rough terrain of the southwest.

After a rocky beginning and plenty of mistakes, you've developed into a fairly proficient outdoorsman. You've learned to savor the taste of cactus fruits and coyote meat. You've also developed the most important desert survival skill, which is a knack for locating water. You observe the flight patterns of birds, stay close to water-dependent plants, and spend every morning collecting dew from rocks. It's not an easy living, but beautiful mornings like this one make it all seem worthwhile.

Out of nowhere, the tranquility is disrupted by the sound of a roaring plane overhead. World War II has been raging on now for three years; this is not the first plane you've seen out here in the desert, and it probably won't be the last. You look up and see that it's pretty big—most definitely military. You barely get a look before it speeds away toward the horizon. You don't give the plane much more thought as you start to build a fire; it's time for a little coffee.

Then comes the flash. It's like a bolt of lightning illuminating the sky, a thousand times brighter than full daylight. As the flash fades, you realize you can't see, and you suddenly feel an intense heat burning every square inch of your body. Blind and panicked, you fear that you're somehow engulfed in flames—but before you can react, a blistering gust of wind sweeps you off the ground, sends you flying backward thirty feet, and drops you onto your back.

As you struggle to sit up, you regain your vision just in time to see a brilliant multicolored fireball on the horizon. It's followed by a sound like distant thunder, only louder. The fireball turns to dust and rises in the air like a huge mushroom, billowing at the top and falling over itself.

Talk about being in the wrong place at the wrong time. A nondescript desert in central New Mexico was not the place to be on the morning of July 16, 1945, when the world's first atomic bomb was detonated. The explosion was the equivalent of 18.6 kilotons of TNT; the shock wave shattered windows as far as 120 miles away. The blast created a flash of light that was seen over the entire state of New Mexico—and in parts of Arizona, Texas, and Mexico. The mushroom cloud rose to over 38,000 feet in a few minutes.

The explosion made a ten-foot deep crater that was 24,000 feet across. The surrounding desert sand was melted into a jade-colored solid (similar to glass) that scientists named Trinitite. Today, the site of the explosion is open to visitors twice a year, but it is recommended that small children and pregnant women skip the tour. The radiation levels of the crater are still ten times higher than those in surrounding areas.

Thanks to advanced military technology, no person today could stand being within fifteen miles of a nuclear explosion (the extreme heat would simply burn your flesh away). Modern nuclear weapons can level mountains; a human body would be obliterated in less than a second. A single detonation near Boston could claim the lives of more than a million people instantly, and another million would die later from fatal injuries. An estimated 500,000 would suffer from the lack of adequate medical care.

Sounds grisly, but many scientists say they'd *prefer* to be at ground zero in the event of a nuclear war. That's because everyone else will have to contend with uncontrollable fires, a cloud of smoke blanketing the northern hemisphere, a loss of electric power and communications (due to the electromagnetic pulse), extreme weather conditions, starvation, disease, and probably the near extinction of the human race.

You've unwittingly received a front seat to how it all began—who said life as an outcast and a drifter would never be meaningful? Even though you're 1.5 miles from the epicenter of the blast, the explosion was strong enough to level a building; fortunately, your body is more resilient than concrete. As you lie on the ground, the worst of your injuries appear to be a few bumps and bruises, plus a nasty burn that feels like you've been in the sun too long. A much larger problem is just trying to wrap your mind around what you've experienced. Divine intervention, alien invasion—you'd believe any explanation right about now, no matter how implausible.

You stagger to your feet. You feel okay—a bit sore and bruised, but basically all right. Unfortunately, you have no way of realizing that your bones are filled with excessive amounts of radiation, and this new addition to your body may cause you to develop cancer. Or you might end up just fine. Scientists who have researched the atomic bombings of Hiroshima noticed an increase in breast cancer and lung cancer among the local population. Then again, many survivors appeared to be unharmed. The effects of radiation are truly unpredictable.

It could take years before you become sick—and by the time you do, you might not associate your illness with the event you just witnessed. Right now, you are alone and scared. You gather your things and quickly start walking away from the blast.

After a few miles, you come across a jeep full of military personnel. As soon as they see that you're okay, they make you promise never to tell anyone what you saw. A big brawny guy with a mustache and aviator glasses says, "We know who you are and we can find you. So keep your mouth shut."

That's enough of a warning for you—and you decide to return to civilization before the government drops another bomb in your backyard. Time to get a new dog, find a new job, and look up the ex-wife.

PART III

SOMEBODY GET A DOCTOR

kiss of the defibrillator

kiss of the defibrillator lator

One moment I was sitting contentedly at my computer writing a column. The next I was experiencing sudden severe chest pain. I knew immediately, with horror, that I was suffering an acute coronary attack.

—DR. W. GIFFORD-JONES, ONTARIO, 1998

Your heart is pounding. Torrents of sweat drip off your face. These are both natural responses as your body labors to keep up with a younger coworker, Larry, who's determined to beat you in a racquetball match. He may be stronger and faster, but you're more determined to win—and you're up, two to one. Your heart beats faster, removing carbon dioxide and metabolic waste from your overworked muscles and replacing them with oxygenated blood and fresh nutrients. Of course, you're completely unaware that any of this is happening; you're too busy wondering why your boss passed you over for a promotion—and gave it to an inexperienced, fresh-out-of-school punk like Larry.

You lunge for an overhead smash and barrel into the wall of the court. And just then you feel a sudden and vaguely familiar pain; you immediately stop and sit down. There's a constricting, vise-like feeling around your rib cage and it's so bad you can't even speak; it feels like an elephant is sitting on your chest. The pain radiates down your arm and up into your jaw, like a rapidly spreading poison. Larry has his cell phone out and he's dialing 911. As if in a dream, you can see Larry shouting into the phone, but your view of him is becoming hazy; then you fall backward and everything goes black.

Yes, it's the world's number one killer, chronic heart disease, and the statistics are scary: it's the culprit in one out of every five deaths in America and claims the lives of half a million Americans every year. Every twenty-nine seconds, someone in the United States has a cardiac event, and every minute someone will die from one. Of course, there are many risk factors that lead to heart disease: diet, age, smoking, obesity, hypertension, and genetics. Heart disease creates clots of hard deposits of cholesterol on the artery walls, which limits the amount of blood and oxygen that can flow to the heart muscle. And when that supply gets too low, the result is a *myocardial infarction*, or a heart attack. The heart will beat chaotically (known as *ventricular fibrillation*), and sometimes stop for good.

But when your heart does fibrillate, it's not necessarily fatal. If performed quickly and correctly, CPR (cardio-pulmonary resuscitation) can prolong your life, and a defibrillator can even return your heart to a normal rhythm. But time is of the essence: for every minute that passes after your heart goes into a condition like ventricular fibrillation or stops beating altogether, your chances of survival decrease by ten percent. Do the math, and you'll realize that you have less than ten minutes to receive the proper medical attention—or else.

You've already had one small heart attack, but there was minimal permanent damage to the muscle and you were told not to curb your physical activity. Unfortunately, your desire to kick Larry's ass has precipitated this second, more serious cardiac event. As you race around the court, your adrenal gland secretes adrenaline (it beats an energy bar), but it has an adverse effect as your coronary artery spasms and the diminishing blood supply, known as *ischemia*, causes the pain in your chest. Because of the previous damage done by your first heart attack (the result of arteriosclerosis), the ischemia quickly leads to an irregular rhythm, or *arrhythmia*, of the heart.

Fortunately for you, Larry has taken a CPR class. (Guess he's not such a punk after all.) He lays you onto your back and, after determining that you are unresponsive and not breathing, he begins the basic steps of cardiopulmonary resuscitation. Larry gently tilts your neck back to clear your airway, pinches your nose, and puts his lips over yours. He then blows two breaths into your lungs. This pushes oxygenated air into your lungs, which allows the oxygen to permeate the linings of your lungs and enter the bloodstream, thus keeping your organs and brain alive.

Larry begins chest compressions by clasping his hand and pressing your chest at the base of the sternum. The resulting pressure pushes blood through the arteries to the brain and other organs. When Larry releases, the pressure drops, and blood flows back into the heart from the veins. On rare occasions, your heart will automatically regain a proper rhythm on its own, so after fifteen compressions, Larry checks your pulse and listens for sounds of breathing. When he hears neither, he gives you an additional two breaths and repeats the compressions.

In the meantime, you are unconscious and aware of nothing. Of course, you're also dying, and the longer you stay unconscious, the more likely it is you will remain that way. When the paramedics come racing across the racquetball court, there is still no change in your condition. They rip off your T-shirt and attach three leads from a portable heart monitor. The readings are all over the place—the single green line is chaotically spiking and falling, which shows that your heart is still in ventricular fibrillation.

One of the paramedics snakes a breathing tube down your windpipe; another connects the opposite end of the tube to the reservoir of an oxygen tank, which delivers the much-needed oxygen to your lungs. Still another paramedic has connected you to an IV that is slowly releasing drugs into your bloodstream; these medications will help control the rhythm of your heart and strengthen the force of contraction.

Next, the defibrillator is charged. The metal paddles are smeared with a gel to protect your skin from burning, and then a paramedic presses them against your chest. She yells "Clear!" and her companions, knowing the drill, take two full steps backward—they don't want to be anywhere near you when the jolt is delivered, because your flailing arms and legs could transfer the voltage. For twenty-thousandths of a second, your body is shocked with 2,000 volts of electricity. This is the same amount of electricity you would receive if you stuck your finger in a wall socket and left it there for five minutes. Ironically, this massive jolt actually stops the heart dead in its tracks—but only for a moment, and then the body prompts the heart to resume its own natural rhythm.

On the monitor, the pulsing green line is now rising and falling in a controlled pattern, reflecting the natural beating of your heart. You're now breathing on your own and have a pulse, but you're still unconscious. The paramedics load you onto the ambulance so you can receive treatment at the hospital, where doctors will determine exactly what happened to your heart. Hours later, you awaken in a hospital bed, feeling much better than you'd expect. You don't remember the ambulance ride, the jolt of the defibrillator, or the visit from the paramedics. In fact, the only thing you do remember is your last desperate smash on the racquetball court, and you ask the nurse on duty if she has any idea who won the point.

three days of detox

> Your intestines start squirming and twisting like worms
> until you can't stand it anymore.
>
> —AN ANONYMOUS HEROIN USER IN DETOX, SEATTLE, 1997

After your last hit wears off, you feel exhausted and collapse into a deep, restful sleep. Unfortunately, you awaken from this sleep after just two hours, because your brain is already craving another hit. Your eyes are watering and your pupils are dilated. Your nose runs like you have a bad head cold, and the sneezing fits are uncontrollable.

As lead singer of the hair metal band Mousse and Roses, you party all night, sleep all day, and don't know the meaning of the word "health-conscious." Most of your year is spent in tour buses and hotel rooms, where you indulge in overpriced room service and underage female fans. You drink whiskey like tap water and dabble in a number of illicit substances—most recently, heroin, which your drummer buys cheap from his nephew in Nevada. You still have enough smack to last you for another three days, but an urgent phone call from your manager inspires you to flush your entire supply down the toilet.

You've been invited to appear on VH1's *Behind the Music*, and the first interview is supposed to tape in just ten days. Over the last few years, M&R's album sales have been sagging, and this interview could be a great way to boost the band's visibility. But a quick glance in the mirror confirms that you're not ready for prime time—you look like death warmed over. And there's no time for rehab, so your only option is to go cold turkey. You hang the "Do Not Disturb" sign on the doorknob of your hotel room, and then hunker down for a very long seventy-two hours.

Heroin is, of course, an illegal drug made from the opium poppy, a plant found in the Middle East, Southeast Asia, and parts of Central and South America. More than 330 tons of heroin are produced and sold every year. In 1998, Americans spent $11.6 billion on the drug— which is more than they spent on movie tickets, concert tickets, and theater tickets combined. But for all the money involved, heroin's production process is decidedly unglamorous. Drug farmers collect the sap from the seeds of the opium poppy, and then dry it to form a gum that is later washed. The result is opium. A chemical process further refines the opium to create heroin, which is about forty times more powerful.

In the United States, it has been estimated that 2.4 million people have tried heroin at some point in their lives, and almost 100,000 new users try the drug every year. Whether smoked, snorted, or injected, heroin acts in a manner that is similar to the body's own natural endorphins. The heroin molecules travel to nerve endings in the brain, lock onto the endorphin-receptor sites, and block the space between nerve cells that normally acts as a communication hub. This action inhibits neurons that control mood, movement, and physiology from firing, and results in a pain-free and euphoric effect.

That's the high, but this is the low: Over months of continuous usage, your body has become dependent on the drug. As soon as you stop, your long-inhibited neurons resume the production of neurotransmitters. Since your body has long adapted to the presence of the drug, this leads to an imbalance of chemicals in your brain—and withdrawal effects ranging from headaches and cramps to chills and muscle spasms.

You've heard all kinds of detox horror stories so at least you're expecting the worst. You curl up in bed and manage to sleep for an hour—but then you wake up feeling terribly anxious. Your sheets are soaked with sweat, and you can't stop tossing and turning. This restlessness is just another way for your body to explain that it wants another fix.

Your hotel room offers very few diversions from your suffering. Even the cable television is little consolation. You rummage around for something to read but all you can find is a Bible; you skim through a few pages of the Old Testament but the story is kind of slow and you can't get into it. You feel increasingly weak, listless, uncomfortable, and irritable. When the other members of your band knock on the door, you shout that you don't want to be disturbed. When the phone rings, you don't answer it.

At dinner time, you consider ordering food, but just glancing at the room service menu makes you want to hurl. You can't even keep water down. You flip on VH1 and watch an interview with Mick Redbone, the washed-up lead singer of a popular '70s rock band. Redbone is sitting in a dark studio, wearing sunglasses, and has trouble answering simple yes or no questions. Watching him strengthens your resolve. You don't want to look like Mick Redbone. You're going to kick this habit once and for all.

By day two, everything hurts. It hurts to move. It hurts to sit down. It hurts to stand up. Even your clothes hurt. And it's not a dull ache, but a severe pain that emanates through your muscle and settles deep in your bones. You feel like you're going to die, but the pain isn't nearly that severe. Your mind makes you feel like you're suffering much more than you actually are. And the worst part is, you know you can end the pain just by walking down the hallway, knocking on the door to your drummer's room, and asking him for a hit.

Anything that even touches your skin elicits a wave of agony, like you're covered with open sores. Up until recently, the narcotics were dulling your nerves—and in your current drug-free condition, these nerves are newly sensitized. You're completely exhausted and your body shivers uncontrollably—just another effect of those misplaced neurotransmitters. You get up and look at the thermostat, but it reads seventy-eight degrees. How can you be so cold?

By the morning of day three, your whole gastrointestinal system is in turmoil. You barely make it to the bathroom before the diarrhea hits. It's on the toilet that you start to cry uncontrollably. You don't want to go on *Behind the Music* anymore. You don't want to spend another minute in this lousy hotel room. You wish you were back in 1988 again, when the whole country loved you and the band ended up on the cover of *Rolling Stone* magazine.

This is your lowest point. The symptoms begin to ebb over the next few days, and on the morning of day five, you actually go down to the hotel lobby for the complimentary breakfast. You manage to eat half of a bagel and drink a little orange juice. The food feels good in your system, and you start collecting your thoughts for that VH1 interview.

Then your drummer enters the lobby. He seems surprised to see you, then winks and explains, "My nephew in Nevada sent us a little care package yesterday." The idea of getting high is surprisingly tempting right now; in fact, rehab counselors estimate that one in five recovering heroin addicts will eventually fall back into their old habits. But for now the odds are still on your side—just say, "Oh, no."

meat your maker

I'm going crazy! I have mad-cow disease!

—ARNAUD EBOLI, 17, VICTIM OF MAD COW DISEASE IN
FRANCE, 2000

Your true passion is meat, all different kinds of meat: prime rib, filet mignon, beef stew, sirloin steak, salisbury steak, burgers, hot dogs, you name it. You love your beef and you love it best when it's cooked rare, the same way your family has served it for generations. But your passion for bloody animal flesh has now led to the onset of some truly bizarre physical symptoms.

The slurring of speech was one thing. The depression. The emotional outbursts. The aches and pains. All of it could be justified—your family assumed that you were simply "stressed about work." But then comes the first day you can't feed yourself—the day you spear a meatball with your fork, lift it toward your mouth, and press it repeatedly into your cheek. Your loved ones bring you to the hospital emergency room, fearful that you might be having a nervous breakdown.

The doctors run a battery of tests. At first, everything appears to be in order. The brain scan looks normal. The MRI also looks good. But the *electroencephalograph*, a device which measures brain wave activity, reveals an abnormal pattern. The symptoms and findings point to Creutzfeldt-Jakob disease (CJD), which your family has never heard of. But they are familiar with mad cow disease, and they're dismayed to learn that you're suffering from the human equivalent.

Mad cow disease first entered the world's consciousness in 1986. That year, several British farmers noticed some of their cows were losing weight, walking strangely, and isolating themselves from the rest of the herd. These cows died prematurely, and autopsies showed that the animals' brains had tiny microscopic holes, like a sponge. The disease was officially named bovine spongiform encephalopathy (BSE).

BSE is similar to a disease called scrapie, which farmers have known about for more than one hundred years. Scrapie affects sheep the way BSE affects cows—and it's believed that scrapie spread to cows after cattle were fed a protein supplement made of tainted sheep offal (the leftovers of butchered animals). In the '90s, the spread of BSE (now popularly known as mad cow disease) approached epidemic proportions throughout Britain. By 1993, scientists were reporting more than 1,000 cases per week, although incidents have been on the decline since the government banned the use of cattle and sheep offal.

According to the World Health Organization, 113 cases of Creutzfeldt-Jakob disease have been reported worldwide since the mid-1990s; most have occurred in Britain. This disease, which also causes sponge-like holes in the brain, has been linked to mad cow disease. No one knows how the disease passes from cows to humans, but scientists have speculated about a number of different theories.

Here's one likely version of events: At your local slaughterhouse, the cows are stunned, and then a steel rod is plunged through the animal's brain and into its spinal cord, to stop the animal from kicking.

This steel rod pierces the membrane around a cow's brain and spills some of the contents on the rest of the animal as it is butchered. Mixed in with this brain matter are funky-looking protein cells called *prions*. Because of their unusual shape, these proteins do not break down easily like other proteins, and they can cause damage to otherwise normal cells.

When you ingest your beloved T-bone steak (or cheese steak, or minute steak) these prions can enter your bloodstream, accumulate in your lymph nodes, spleen, and other organs, and eventually wind up in your brain, where they can wreak havoc. This process takes a long time; it is believed the incubation period for CJD is anywhere from ten to forty years. No one knows if it's caused by a lifetime of eating meat or a single bad burger. But regardless of the cause, the problem is very real: when enough prions accumulate in your brain, they'll start to kill other healthy cells by boring through your brain like termites in a wood floor.

The degenerative process starts slowly, but accelerates quickly. In the early weeks, you have difficulty sleeping, and occasionally forget minor things, like the location of your house keys. You assume that your problems are emotional, but visits to psychiatrists only make you feel more anxious and confused. Sometimes you feel twinges of pain in various parts of your body. Sometimes you just want to scream. You're finding it hard to communicate with your family, and you spend a lot of time in your bedroom, so you won't have to see or speak to anyone.

Several months pass before you finally stab yourself in the face with that meatball. Unfortunately, by the time your doctors mention the possibility of CJD, you can barely comprehend what they're talking about. The doctors explain to your family that there is no real way to diagnose CJD until your brain can be examined in an autopsy (where, presumably, it would reveal a series of sponge-like holes). For now, they're recommending hospitalization and constant observation.

As you lie in your bed, oblivious to friends and family standing vigil, more and more of your bodily functions fail. Eventually, you drop into a semiconscious haze. It's a matter of days before you can't breathe on your own, and the doctors put you on life support.

At this point, you are virtually in a coma. Eight months after your initial symptoms, your heart stops beating.

Your family is grieving but it's possible that they haven't completely accepted the gravity of the situation; at the dinner following your funeral service, the most popular entrée on the buffet table is your Aunt Edna's meat pies.

amputation, civil war style

amputation civil war style

Houses and barns, but chiefly the woods were used as hospitals, and the wounded, necessarily endured much suffering.

—DR. JONATHAN LETTERMAN, MEDICAL DIRECTOR, ARMY OF THE POTOMAC, 1862

It's the bloody Battle of Antietam and your kneecap took a direct hit. Damn those Union bastards—if you ever get back out there, you're gonna kill a few to pay for this. That's *if* you ever get back out there. Your knee is basically shattered, and the surgeon makes a quick determination—after probing the wound with his finger. "All right, this leg's coming off—the quicker, the better." You are delirious from the pain, but you know enough to fear the implications of a battlefield amputation. Thanks to the heavy number of casualties, your surgeon has been amputating arms and legs all day, and the proof is a four-foot pile of bloody limbs arranged haphazardly in the corner of the tent. To make matters worse, they're also out of chloroform.

During the American Civil War the surgeons used a pretty simple rule of thumb for battlefield wound triage: If it's busted, cut it off. Amputations were extremely common in the bloody conflict; in fact, three out of four surgical procedures performed during the war were amputations. In the Union army alone, more than 30,000 limbs were lopped off.

On the battlefield of the 1860s, surgery wasn't the most antiseptic of activities. Blood-and-pus-splattered doctors performed multiple procedures, often without even rinsing their hands in between. (Infection and its causes were largely misunderstood at that time.) Sponges were reused after simply being rinsed in available bloody water. Instruments were quickly wiped down before digging into the next patient's flesh. And if a knife was dropped onto the dirt floor, it was often just wiped off and reused.

In spite of all this, Civil War amputations were not a complete horror show. In most cases, a primitive form of anesthesia was available. The surgeon soaked a rag in chloroform and placed it into the patient's mouth, rendering him basically senseless for the duration. (The trick is knowing when to remove the rag—chloroform poisoning would kill faster than gangrene.) But even with the anesthesia, the patient would eventually wake up, and infection was pretty much par for the course.

Confederate losses were heavy as General Lee attempted an invasion of the North and was intercepted in Maryland. During a charge, you were intercepted by a Minié ball, a large, heavy bullet that was fired by a Union soldier's musket and smashed through your kneecap. The pain is excruciating, but when you hear the surgeon's diagnosis, you know the worst is yet to come.

The surgeon's assistant secures you to a makeshift operating table (basically, a wooden plank placed atop two sawhorses). A tourniquet is tied around the top of your thigh, cutting off the flow of blood through your femoral artery. The cinch of the tightly drawn cloth puts pressure on the femoral nerve, and you start to struggle. Two more assistants are called over to help hold you down. One of them places a small lead bullet in your mouth (it's not just an expression!) so you can bite down and divert your attention away from your leg.

The surgeon takes a bloody scalpel and makes an incision above your knee, slicing through the skin and into the quadriceps. As the blade enters, severing nerve fibers along the way, the pain is a flash of white-hot searing agony, moving like a wave across your thigh. You groan and make an inhuman noise. You clamp your teeth down on the bullet but it doesn't help. The surgeon cuts almost completely around the leg to the hamstring muscle in the back, leaving just a small flap of skin on one side.

When the surgeon lifts the knife away from your leg, you're granted a temporary respite from the agony—until you catch a glimpse of the hacksaw. Fortunately, you're not close enough to see that its once-razor-sharp teeth have been dulled by the day's activity.

The surgeon places the saw on the femur and quickly moves it back and forth against the bone. As he cuts, it's not the feeling but the sound that drives you really mad—a heavy, scraping noise that results from dull metal gnawing through your bone. Your heart speeds up again, your blood pressure drops, and shock slows the supply of oxygenated blood to your brain. Thankfully, you lose consciousness.

You return to semiconsciousness to see things literally being wrapped up. After sawing through your bone and removing the leg, the surgeon sewed the ends of the arteries with horsehair, and then scraped the end and edges of the bone smooth, so that it would not work its way back through the skin. When the surgeon made his first incision, fifteen painful minutes earlier, he was careful to leave a small flap of skin at the base of the cut. The surgeon pulls this flap across your new stump and swiftly sews it closed—minus a small drainage hole for pus.

Even in your semiconscious state, you feel a sense of relief that the procedure is over. Somebody finds a bottle of whiskey and forces the liquid in your mouth. The effects of the alcohol are temporary, but right now you'll take what you can get. Damn Yankees!

pass the kidney stones, please

It felt like a large, rabid walrus had bitten me in the side.

—W. BRUCE CAMERON, DENVER NEWSPAPER COLUMNIST, 2000

You're driving home from the office when you feel a strange new pain in your lower back. How odd, you think to yourself—even with that new astronomically expensive Aeron desk chair, you still can't escape an occasional nagging backache. You adjust your car seat and rub the sensitive area; it seems to be near the bottom of your back, just above your pelvis. The pain bothers you all the way home. Once inside your house, you head straight for the medicine cabinet and gobble up a few aspirin, hoping for relief.

It doesn't come. After a few hours of lying immobile on the couch, the pain becomes much worse and starts to feel more focused. You begin to doubt that it's muscular and briefly consider appendicitis.

But isn't your appendix in the front? You're not sure. This pain definitely started in your back, but now it feels like it's in your side, and slowly radiating toward your groin. What's over there? you wonder.

What are "over there" are your kidneys—and you are on an express train bound for destination pain. You've got kidney stones, a condition routinely cited as one of the most painful experiences a healthy person can suffer—akin to childbirth. And it's not uncommon: In the United States alone, about five and a half million people are diagnosed with kidney stones each year. It can happen to anyone, but for reasons unknown, men are more susceptible than women.

The stones are hard deposits of chemicals that are produced by the kidneys. The scientific name for them is *nephrolithiasis,* and they are thought to form for any number of reasons (including chemical imbalance, chronic dehydration, local infection, and even genetic predisposition).

There are several different kinds of stones, but the most common ones consist of *calcium oxalate.* These stones form when calcium combines with oxalate, a by-product of substances normally broken down by the kidneys, and they make a hard substance that cannot be dissolved. Often a stone will remain lodged in the kidneys for years, but once it's on the move—watch out.

Your invader is being drawn from your kidney by a combination of gravity and urine. As soon as the stone begins moving inside your kidneys, you get that first sensation of pain. The kidney stone is a spiky, solid object about the size of a tomato seed—but this tiny torment is bumping into extremely sensitive tissue that is accustomed to contact with liquids, not solids.

When you feel the pain radiating toward your groin, it's because that's the actual direction in which the stone is moving. After months of gestation in the kidneys, it's heading toward your ureter, a tube-like structure that carries urine to the bladder. As the tube stretches to expel the obstruction, the cramping of the tube's muscular walls causes an intense stabbing pain.

When you urinate, the pain is even worse—a nasty burning sensation that nearly brings you to your knees. You now realize something bad is happening in your most "sensitive" region and you shouldn't mess around. An hour later, you're at the hospital, and the doc has diagnosed kidney stones.

There are several methods for treating your condition. Some doctors would use lasers or sound waves to break up the stones. As a last resort, there's also invasive surgery (in which a catheter is inserted through the urethra and a hook device snares and removes the blockage). In your case, the stone is small enough that you can "pass it" yourself—but the next leg of its journey is by far the worst.

As you lie in your hospital bed—just twelve hours after those first nagging signs of a backache—you feel a pain that is at least a million times worse than anything you have ever experienced in your life. It's like someone is using a knife to carve you like a pumpkin from the inside.

In actuality, the stone is passing from the ureter into the bladder, and the pain results from the stone nudging through a tiny valve that separates the two organs. You are given plenty of fluids to flush the intruder along—plus some Demerol that helps you deal with the pain.

Now it's a waiting game. Your doctor explains that the worst is actually over, because your bladder is less sensitive than the ureter. But you still have your doubts—in your imagination, the stone is the size of a golf ball, and its final destination is a very tiny (and very sensitive!) opening. To take your mind off the inevitable pain, you flip on the television and try to watch a game show. But every time you take another sip of water, you know you're taking another step closer to finally passing the stone.

On your next—and final—visit to the bathroom, a nurse gives you an object that resembles a coffee filter. You're instructed to urinate in it so that you can catch your "friend." As the muscles of your bladder relax, you feel the familiar pain one last time and sure enough, the stone splashes out in a stream of urine, landing in the filter with a tiny ping (and looking much smaller than the huge spiked golf ball you imagined).

You're instantly relieved and feel rather proud of yourself for surviving the ordeal. But as you dress yourself, your doctor informs you that, having developed one kidney stone, you now have an increased susceptibility to future kidney stones. Thanks for the info, doc!

ebolapalooza

I never thought about dying. I was so sick I couldn't think about anything.

—CECILIA AMWECH, A (VERY RARE) SURVIVOR OF EBOLA,
UGANDA, 2000

Luckily, you're unconscious. Unfortunately, the people around you are not. Horror films don't do justice to this kind of grotesque display. Blood is leaking—no, *pouring*—out of your nose. The deep red liquid is welling up out of your eye sockets. It's draining from virtually every orifice in your body, dripping over your ragged hospital gown, and soaking into the battered mattress. Less than two weeks ago, you were an engineer for one of the most profitable mining companies in the United States—but a tiny microscopic predator is wreaking havoc on your body, and it's not finished with you yet.

First discovered in 1976, the Ebola virus was named for a river in Zaire (now the Democratic Republic of the Congo), near the site of the initial outbreak. The virus has appeared sporadically since then, killing ninety percent of those it infects. The origins of Ebola are not known, but it is believed to be an animal-borne disease spread by incidental contact with bodily fluids to their human caretakers. Humans are not a natural host for the virus, but it is so contagious that each recent occurence of the disease has led to a serious outbreak in Africa—on four separate occasions, it has killed hundreds.

Ebola is a member of a family of RNA viruses called the *Filoviridae*. The name comes from the Latin term for "thread-like." Under the microscope, the virus looks quite similar to a thread with a loop that resembles a noose. This ominous-looking virus destroys healthy cells and kills its host before the body's immune system has any chance of retaliating. There is no known cure.

Although there has yet to be an Ebola outbreak outside of central Africa, the virus has traveled all the way to the United States at least once. In 1989, a portion of a shipment of monkeys from the Philippines mysteriously died in a holding facility in a suburb of Washington, D.C. It was later determined that the cause of death was Ebola. What makes the incident even more frightening is the fact that several of the monkeys were not in contact with each other, which means the disease was spread through the air. Fortunately, this strain of the Ebola virus was not harmful to humans; in another misplaced shipment, the United States might not be so lucky.

When you embarked for Africa less than a month ago, you knew you were exposing yourself to any number of deadly diseases. But your superiors at Lifeline, an Indiana-based mining company, were concerned about your safety, and they sent you to a company doctor who gave you countless immunizations and vaccinations. As Lifeline's top engineer, your assignment is to scout a new location for a copper mine deep in the jungles of the Congo.

In order to negotiate land rights, your party visits a village that is on the proposed site. When you arrive, locals explain that their leader is sick, and they bring you to meet him in a makeshift hospital. When the members of your party see his condition, everyone is aghast. The tribal leader is extremely pale and thin. His eyes are red and there are streaks of blood at the corners of his mouth. You and your team stay just long enough to not appear disrespectful—and then hurry far, far away, fearing the risks of exposure to whatever he is suffering from.

You explain the situation to Lifeline corporate headquarters, and the top brass fire back an urgent message telling you to return home immediately—they're going to send medical relief to the area before making any further inroads. A week later, you're flying back to New York. By the end of the first in-flight movie, you've got a killer migraine. Next to you in the window seat is a jovial English business-man who insists that a quick nip of Scotch will cure your headache—and he insists that you take a swig from his glass. It just makes your headache worse.

By the time you land at Kennedy Airport, your throat is sore and your muscles ache all over. Even with the memory of the village elder fresh in your mind, you attribute these symptoms to air travel and too many sixteen-hour workdays. You stay home in bed and try to wait it out. But twenty-four hours later, you're vomiting a dark reddish-black liquid and expelling bloody diarrhea.

The Ebola virus takes about seven days to incubate—and that's nearly exactly how much time has elapsed since you left the tribal leader's makeshift hospital bed. Now the virus is invading cells throughout your body and causing them to burst. Especially vulnerable are the *endothelial* cells that line the interior of your veins and arteries. At the same time, Ebola disables your immune system, which would normally fend off a viral invader. (Scientists still aren't sure how it accomplishes this.) The Ebola virus also subverts your cells' genetic machinery and duplicates itself. All over your body, the quickly repli-cating virus is destroying healthy cells.

You have the wherewithal to call an ambulance—and when the para-medics arrive, you tell them you've been working in Africa. You are rushed to a contamination unit at a nearby hospital, where you are completely quarantined and treated by doctors in biohazard suits.

You are given intravenous fluids and a blood transfusion, but these actions only serve to delay the inevitable. Ruptured cells are spilling their contents into neighboring tissue and creating grotesque raised rashes over your entire body. The pain feels hot and intense on the surface of your skin, and there's a burning sensation deep inside your chest. The doctors try to give you enough medication to make you comfortable, but that's about all they can do.

Your body is slowly dying, one cell at a time. Soon, the lining of your gastrointestinal tract becomes so weak from disintegration that blood pools in your bowels and begins to drain from your rectum, taking pieces of your intestines with it. Your weakened arteries can't pump enough blood to your brain, and everything goes dark.

Minutes after you lose consciousness, your falling blood pressure leaves your circulatory system unable to pump blood to any of your vital organs. The mucous membranes of your body—including your eyes, ears, and nose—begin to bleed. Compounding this severe bleeding is your body's inability to clot (thanks to the total failure of your immune system). You bleed to death in the hospital only a few days after returning from your business trip.

As a pair of orderlies wheel you out of the hospital, two paramedics are wheeling in a not-so-jovial English businessman with a flask of Scotch in his jacket pocket. "It's so strange," he's telling the paramedics. "I've only been in the United States for seven days, but I've started feeling the queerest aches and pains . . ."

PART IV

CRIME AND PUNISHMENT

caught in the crossfire

caught in the crossfire

**The bullet hit me so hard I fell to the ground. The first
bullet hit me—that's what I think—in the stomach, on the
left. It was just darkness.**

—MEEKA JOHNSON, GUNSHOT VICTIM IN CHICAGO, 1991

Pop, pop, pop. You could swear the sound is just some kids shooting
off fireworks. After all, you're walking through a crowded fair on a
downtown city street, and the atmosphere is pretty festive. *Pop, pop,
pop.* There it goes again, but everyone around you just carries on,
business as usual. Then comes the commotion. People start running;
there are a few screams and the streets clear. Through the mayhem,
you see two young men tearing down the sidewalk. One appears to be
chasing the other. Again that sound: *Pop, pop, pop.* This time you feel
something hit you in the shoulder. Are those guys throwing stones at

each other? Did a rock just hit you? It's not until you actually see the glint of a gun in the crowd that it occurs to you: You've been shot.

It happens. In the United States, it's fair to say it happens relatively often. There are an estimated 211 million firearms in America—nearly one for every person. Those guns cause around 40,000 firearm deaths per year and almost 120,000 nonfatal injuries. The only good news to draw from these statistics is that getting shot is not *necessarily* fatal. In fact, your chances of survival are pretty good, if the bullet doesn't come near the brain, spinal cord, or a major organ.

The bad news is that an injury from a gunshot can happen almost anywhere. From the home to the street to the car, you're never completely safe. And because a gun by definition shoots a projectile into the air, there is always the possibility of being unwittingly caught in the crossfire.

Take, for example, a street fair where a stupid argument over who pays for a funnel cake erupts into a full-blown shootout. After you realize that you may have been shot, you reach for your shoulder. What you feel is squishy and sticky, and it is in fact a gaping hole in the tissue just below your collarbone. Up to this point, you haven't experienced any pain because (in one of those mysterious acts of the brain), you hadn't realized you were shot. Now, after touching the wound, and in effect sobering up a bit, the hot, burning pain arrives. Your brain begins to acknowledge the signal, transmitted by the nociceptors in the ruptured tissue in your shoulder.

Meanwhile, the .38 bullet lodged inside you has enjoyed a pretty wild ride itself. Once inside the body, bullets do not continue traveling in any predictable direction; rather, they ricochet off bones and organs, losing their shape along the way, and can bounce around the body like a pinball. (Although .38s and .45s are the big guns of choice in urban areas, most pathologists agree that .22 slugs are among the most destructive; it's not uncommon to hear of .22 slugs that enter the body through the lower back and somehow zigzag their way up and out through the right shoulder.)

When the bullet first enters your body, it tears through skin and then the pectoral muscle. Fortunately, the bullet misses, although not by much, both the *carotid* and *brachial* arteries—both of which could have ruptured, leading to major blood loss and a fairly swift death. Instead, it opens a hole in the muscle and nicks the clavicle bone, sending tiny shards of bone matter into the surrounding soft tissue. Luckily, the slug stops its forward motion before exiting the body through the back. (Exit wounds can be a lot messier than entry wounds.)

As it passed through your body, the .38 has created a cavity as it destroys tissue in its wake. If you were able to watch the bullet in slow motion, you would see an even bigger cavity created by the displacement of tissue, due to the kinetic energy created by the movement of the bullet. This temporary cavity returns to shape, like a sponge. The elasticity of the body actually prevents a lot of further damage.

There will be blood loss, and countless cells have been ruptured by the path of the bullet; these cells spill their content into the surrounding tissue, and the result is an intense, burning pain. But even more painful are the splintered shards of bone, which scratch against and often pierce the surrounding tissue, muscles, and blood vessels. The combination of so many pain signals make the wound feel even larger than it is—and to make matters worse, infection is still a possibility. The bullet itself is sterile due to the heat produced upon firing, but the bits of clothing, hair, and skin it picked up upon entry are not.

After the pain hits, you fall backward. This is essentially a learned behavior: Television and movies have taught us that when we're shot, we fall down. But for a bullet to actually knock a person off his feet, physics dictates that the shooter would also need to fall over. Of course, you're not considering these conundrums right now—you just want to get some help.

Strangers quickly surround you. Someone yells, "We need an ambulance! Somebody get an ambulance!" Fifteen cell phones come out and everybody calls 911. You figure you're going to be all right, but the pain and the loss of blood have left you in a mild state of shock; as your blood pressure continues to drop, you feel a little dazed. Another person yells, "Bring us some water!" But even in your semiconscious state, you're thinking you'd really prefer one of those funnel cakes . . .

ol' sparky

My mouth tasted like cold peanut butter. I felt a burning in my head and my left leg, and I jumped against the straps.

—WILLIE FRANCIS, ELECTRIC CHAIR SURVIVOR, LOUISIANA, 1946

You struggled with the decision for days but eventually came up with the perfect last meal: Three scrambled eggs, one bowl of creamed corn, one pound of fried bacon, one bag of Lay's Sour Cream and Onion Potato Chips, one quart of peanut butter ice cream, and one very well-done T-bone steak. To your astonishment, you get everything you ask for. (With the exception of cigarettes and booze, prisoners ordering their last meal can usually request and receive just about anything.) You eat all of the food with gusto, and your only complaint is that the steak is served medium rare, not well done—but at this point, salmonella is the least of your worries. In just two hours from now, you're going to experience some 2,000 volts coursing through your entire body. Leave it to a dentist to come up with a new method of inflicting pain. In 1881, one named Alfred P. Southwick proposed the concept for the electric chair after watching a vagrant in Buffalo, New York, stumble into a street light transformer. By 1890, New York became the first state to use the chair as a method of capital punishment with the execution of convicted killer William Kemmler. Since then, more than 4,000 people have been put to death using the electric chair in the United States. (The Philippines is the only country outside the U.S. to ever use it.)

Alfred P. Southwick developed the electric chair as a pain-free alternative to hanging, which he considered to be a cruel and inhumane punishment (a botched hanging can result in slow strangulation or even decapitation). But the electric chair can be a horror show in its own way. Over the last century, a number of people have been lucky (or unlucky) enough to "survive" the electric chair. The first to do so in 1946 described the pain as unbearable. Poor Willie Francis, a condemned prisoner in Lousiana, sat down in a chair with a faulty hookup that led to a weakened electrical current; when the jolt finally came, Francis groaned, jumped, and lifted his chair off the ground. "I'm not dying," Francis shouted to his executioners. Years later, after a failed appeal, Francis found himself back in an electric chair, and this one functioned properly.

Witnesses to electrocutions have reported that victims will vomit, bleed, drool, urinate, and defecate. Sometimes their heads catch fire, and multiple jolts of electricity are often required to kill the prisoner. In recent years, most states have replaced the electric chair with lethal injection, a less violent form of execution. But Old Sparky is far from obsolete: Since capital punishment was reinstated in 1977, 148 men and one woman have been electrocuted. If you commit a serious crime in Nebraska, Georgia, or Alabama (the three states where electrocution is the mandatory form of capital punishment), you risk facing an electric jolt that is literally heart-stopping.

There's no denying that your crime was serious—even if you didn't mean for anyone to get hurt. You've always had an affinity for building bombs, and you didn't think anyone worked in your office building late at night. Unfortunately, you forgot about the custodial staff that came through every Wednesday evening—and now, thanks to you, three people have perished in a fiery inferno. When the day of your execution finally arrives, you're surprised that you feel relief. You've already made peace with yourself and your maker and now it's time to prepare mentally for what you may or may not feel in that chair.

Earlier in the afternoon, one of the prison's medics entered your cell to shave your head as well as the calf of your right leg (you'll find out why later). You changed into a prison uniform that was free of metal clasps and zippers that might conduct electricity. After finishing your last meal, you spent a few minutes glancing around your cell; after spending the last eight years in a space, it's hard to believe that you'll never see it again. Your belongings are packed in a cardboard box that will be shipped to your family at the end of the night—except for a few packs of cigarettes, which you are bequeathing to fellow inmates on death row.

Your execution is scheduled for 10:00 P.M. sharp, and you're served your last meal two hours beforehand. When you're finished, you are offered and accept ten milligrams of Valium. The drug augments the action of neurotransmitter inhibitors in your brain, and your stress is replaced by a feeling of relative well-being. Suddenly, the execution doesn't seem so serious anymore; it feels like more of an inconvenience than anything else.

Once the medication has taken effect, the warden comes to your cell, accompanied by three correction officers. "It's time," he says, and you're too disoriented to stand up. The officers help you to your feet and begin walking you to the death chamber. It's a small gray room with cinder-block walls and a large wooden chair in the center of the room. One wall features a large plate-glass window, and you can see three rows of folding chairs behind it, where some men and women in suits are scribbling notes or just watching. You recognize some of them from your trial—lawyers and journalists. At your request, all of your friends and family agreed to not watch the execution.

You are placed in the chair and your forearms, ankles, waist, chest, and head are tightly secured. A well-worn leather mask is placed over your face, leaving only your nose exposed. Then two electrodes are placed upon your body. The first is attached to a metal receptacle that's encased in a leather shell and rests on top of your head. The second is attached to your hairless right calf. Two electrodes are necessary to complete the circuit; they enable electricity to flow through your body, rather than just into it.

A sponge is then dipped in water and placed on top of your head, underneath the leather cap. Despite all the high-tech electronic equipment, a simple sponge is probably the most important element of the process—the extra water aids conductivity of the electricity and minimizes the length of time it actually takes you to die. You want it to be very wet, and (strangely enough) you also want it to be natural, not synthetic. At a botched electrocution in Florida, where flames engulfed the condemned man's head, it was theorized that the pyrotechnics were the result of a synthetic sponge.

You are now alone in the room; the guards and executioner have left. It is eerily quiet. In the last moment, you swallow hard one final time. Then the warden pushes a small button that completes the circuit, allowing 2,200 volts to begin flowing through your body for a duration of thirty seconds. (That's twenty times the amount of electricity in a common wall outlet.)

You feel a surge of pain that rips through your body from your head to your leg. It feels worst in your arms, back, chest, and legs. Virtually all of your muscles convulse and the current sends them into acute contractions. You arch your back and strain against the straps. As the current passes through the cardiac center in the brain's medulla, it arrests your heart. The high voltage kills the brain by massive depolarization of the brain and brain stem's neural structure, which has the effect of a light switch going off in your mind.

Two subsequent jolts are administered shortly after the first, and this time the current literally bakes your organs; your internal temperature rises to 138 degrees. Blood leaks from your ears and your eyes are blown out of their sockets. Your flesh swells and your skin stretches to the point of breaking; your body turns bright red as its temperature continues to climb.

The lawyers and journalists who witness your demise don't realize any of this. They see your body convulse for a few moments, and then it's all over. The two extra jolts are administered just to be sure that your heart has completely stopped, but in this case they are not necessary—you're already gone. Witnesses can see a small wisp of smoke rising from your head. A doctor stands nearby, waiting to declare you legally dead, but this will not happen for at least three minutes. Right now, you're simply too hot to touch and would blister anyone who makes contact with your skin.

It's safe to assume that somewhere inside your digestive system, that medium-rare steak is now very, very well done.

good to the last drop

good to the last drop drop

Though the terrors of fire are obvious to behold, even from a distance, the potential for cruelty and suffering that lurks in the life-giving force of water is no less devastating.

—MICHAEL KERRIGAN, AUTHOR OF *THE INSTRUMENTS OF TORTURE,* 2001

Your entire body is strapped down. Even your head is immobilized. You can't move a muscle and can't even imagine what kinds of horrors are planned for you. You look up and see that the spigot of a rotting cask is positioned directly over your head. What could it be? Hot oil? Wax? As you writhe against the restraints, your heart flutters in anticipation of what might happen next. Your eyes focus on the spigot and a small droplet of liquid that is hovering at the end of it, ready to drip upon your forehead. You wince and brace yourself as the liquid begins to fall, but nothing actually happens. It's just a tiny drip of cold water.

Of all the torture devices used throughout history, H_2O is perhaps the most commonplace and the most readily available. The most popular application was to force a prisoner to drink. The torturers would hold a victim's mouth open and literally pour in water, forcing the person to swallow it until his belly was engorged to the point of agony. Often the water would be regurgitated, and the prisoner would suffocate.

The Dutch used another variation in the seventeenth century. They would place rags in the victim's mouth and nose, and then douse the head until the rags were saturated—which led to a prompt and efficient suffocation. Another popular technique among the Dutch was the simple dunk. This was performed with an elaborate setup that could repeatedly lift a person and drop him into a body of freezing water.

In American prisons until 1882, inmates were sometimes locked into a shower and sprayed with ice-cold water. But after an accidental death at a prison in New York, the practice was outlawed.

What's happening to you is something much stranger. It has come to be known as Chinese water torture, but was actually invented by a sixteenth-century Italian lawyer named Hippolytus de Marsiliis. (Marsiliis has quite a résumé—see the next chapter on sleep deprivation.) He noticed that drops of water gradually wore away a stone and wondered if they would have the same effect on the human head. The answer is no—but the water can achieve damage of a slightly different variety.

No one knows exactly why this slow drip method has come to be known as Chinese water torture, but escape artist Harry Houdini might have unintentionally coined the phrase in 1903. That year, Houdini introduced the "Chinese Water Torture Cell." It was a stunt in which the escape artist was dropped upside down into a box filled with water. Somewhere along the way, the term "Chinese water torture" was linked to the sixteenth-century Italian procedure.

As an accused heretic in Marsiliis's time, you're about to experience the drip-drip method firsthand. Although you prefer the term scientist to sorcerer, many people seem to think your theories are in direct conflict with the church's teachings. For example, you're convinced that a single drop of human blood is teeming with very tiny moving particles that appear to have lives of their own. Over the last year, you've been trying to construct a "magnifying scope" that would allow a person to view this activity—but with so many interruptions and interrogations by church leaders, progress has been slow.

And now, threatened with a leaky spigot and a rotting cask, you refuse to denounce your beliefs. After all, what are a few drops of water? You endure the "torture" easily for the first fifteen minutes or so, and even chuckle to yourself about its silliness. But soon you find your gaze fixed on the spigot, anxiously awaiting each successive drip. They are spaced out at slow, irregular intervals and you try anything to divert your attention, even closing your eyes. It doesn't take long for the incessant dripping to become incredibly annoying.

As each drop lands on your forehead, nerve receptors in the dermis layer of your skin detect the tiny pressure and relay the signal to your brain. Over and over and over. The water drips down your face and into your eye. It's the erratic nature of the dripping that makes it so torturous; if there were some predictability to the dripping you might be able block out the sensation. But that's not the case. Each drop is followed by a period of waiting and wondering about the next drop.

And sure enough, just a few hours of this slowly starts to drive you mad. It just will not stop. You scream at your torturers, begging them to let you sit up. Your heart is beating faster, your pulse racing. You try to move your head, straining your neck muscles against the straps holding you down. Whatever you do, however you try to divert your mind, you can't escape those drops of water.

You are frantic and you acquiesce. You say you'll denounce everything you believe in if they will only stop the water. You agree that your life's work is akin to witchcraft. You promise to cease your research and devote your life to the church. And after the guards set you free, you keep your end of the bargain—you go home and destroy thousands of hours of microscopic research. It's a course of action that sets science back one hundred years—which just goes to show you shouldn't underestimate the power of a few drops of water.

the third degree

In the end, I didn't know where I was. I was completely
disoriented. I could see people's faces, but I couldn't
remember who they were.

—NEW JERSEY RADIO DJ GLEN JONES, WHO STAYED AWAKE FOR
100 HOURS, 2001

The cops shake you violently and slap you in the face a few times.
You're awake and your eyes are open, but you don't really see anything. You don't hear anything. And you hardly feel anything. You're
like the walking dead. How can you be expected to answer a question
now? Where were you on the night of October 12? Who knows? You
think you're innocent, but you're not even sure. You'd tell the cops
anything at this point, just to go to sleep.

Your tormentors owe a debt of gratitude to Hippolytus de Marsiliis, a lawyer in sixteenth-century Italy who was also the first person to use sleep deprivation as a means of torture. Marsiliis asked his guards to shake the prisoner at random intervals, prick him with a sharp pin, and force him to march around the hallways endlessly. The inevitable disorientation usually led to a confession of some sort, and since then the technique has been practiced by societies around the world.

In seventeenth-century England—where torture per se was forbidden—prisoners were still starved and sleep deprived until they copped to something. In Stalinist Russia, a similar process called "the conveyor system" was used to interrogate prisoners; a series of trained examiners would alternate shifts, asking the same questions of a prisoner again and again. Modern police all over the world have used this tactic, which we generally refer to as the third degree. In the early part of the twentieth century, American cops practiced harsh third-degree interrogations on a regular basis, but those days are fortunately long gone. In 1944, the Supreme Court declared that a defendant not permitted sleep after thirty-six hours of custody was denied "due process of law" (a Fourteenth Amendment constitutional right). And nowadays, most interrogations will rarely last more than six or eight hours; if they go much longer, a public defender has a good shot of convincing a jury that the confession was involuntary (or coerced).

Unfortunately, you're living in harsher, less liberal times—specifically, New York City in 1936, where you've found work as a bellhop in the Plaza Hotel. You were just walking home from work around eleven o' clock in the evening, minding your own business, when a passing police car screeched to a halt. Two cops jumped out, frisked you, and tossed you in the backseat. You have no idea why they've picked you up, but the next morning, your mug will be all over the papers. It turns out that a wealthy socialite back at the Plaza was found with her throat cut—and someone reported that a guy in a hotel uniform was fleeing the scene of the crime.

The two detectives bring you to the Midtown North precinct, cuff you to an uncomfortable wooden chair, and leave you for a few hours in a dimly lit room. There's nothing for you to do except sit and become increasingly irritated by this treatment. When they return, around six in the morning, the two detectives toy with you a bit, ask a few leading questions, and blow some cigarette smoke in your face.

"Look, pal," one of them says, "we don't want to be here all day. Just tell us how you offed the dame so we can make this quick."

"I don't know what you're talking about," you tell them.

"You think she cut her own throat? Is that what happened?"

"I don't know," you tell them. "I have no idea."

That goes on all morning. By noon, you've been awake for thirty hours and you start to feel agitated; accusations of murder are bad enough, but your body is really craving sleep. You feel a bit woozy, like you've had a few too many Irish whiskeys. Cells in your retina send signals to a cluster of nerve cells in your hypothalamus called the *suprachiasmatic nucleus*. These cells are generally referred to as the body's "circadian clock," a system that regulates the body's sleep cycles. The clock instructs your pineal gland to produce *melatonin*, a chemical that lowers your body temperature and makes you feel drowsy. The hypothalamus also regulates your hormone levels and heart rate, to prepare your body for sleep. But just as your body is ready to fall into slumber—whap!—you get another slap to the face, interrupting the natural process and forcing you to remain in this tired, pre-sleep stage.

"Come on, pal," another detective says. "You'll feel a lot better once you get this off your chest."

They continue badgering you for another eighteen hours, taking turns to break up the monotony. By six o'clock the next morning, you've been awake for a full forty-eight hours, and you've completely lost track of time. You ask one of the detectives for the time, but he answers your question with another question: "What time did you step into the dame's hotel room?" You notice he's not even wearing a wristwatch—he must have removed it before entering the room, so you'll stay disoriented.

Around this time, your body starts producing epinephrine, a stimulant that combats the tiredness, and you get a second wind. The result is like a jolt of caffeine. But it's short-lived, only two hours at the most. As you start to slump over, a new pair of detectives shake you and shout in your ears. The torture continues, and over the course of the next day, you meet more than a dozen of New York City's finest, all convinced that you know something about the gorgeous dame in the penthouse suite.

"Let's go over the events of the evening one more time," one of them says, and then he aims a blinding light in your face. As you try to recount the details, they keep interrupting: "And then you got the knife," one says. You deny it. "First you killed her and then you ditched your bloody gloves," says the other. Again, you vehemently deny the statement. "The D.A. wants you to fry for this," they tell you. "We're the only ones who can help you." Your mind is swirling with their accusations.

After eighty hours, you are completely disoriented. When you try to speak, the most you can manage is gibberish. You recognize the faces of your interrogators, but you're not sure if they're the cops who picked you up, or the cops you talked to yesterday. Or maybe today is still yesterday—you don't even know anymore.

"The other bellhops said you came running out of the room," they tell you.

"What bellhops?" you ask. "I don't know bellhops, I don't know any."

While this kind of sleep deprivation certainly qualifies as torture, your life isn't actually in much jeopardy. Lack of sleep will temporarily weaken your immune system, increasing your susceptibility to various illnesses, but many months would need to pass before you finally slip into a coma and die. (This has been known to happen; in Italy there are documented cases of a rare genetic disease called *fatal familial insomnia*, which results in incurable sleep deprivation and finally death).

After ninety-six hours of interrogation—a full four days' worth—you feel like you've been sitting in the same chair for six months. You've sunk into despondency and have stopped responding to the questions. You're not even surprised when the cops uncuff you from the chair and tell you to get the hell out of their precinct. You just stumble out onto Fifty-ninth Street, turn into the nearest alley, lie down, and close your eyes.

For the next fifteen minutes, your eyes roll slowly in circles inside your head as your body sinks into a natural sleep rhythm. Your heart rate and breathing begin to slow. You remain this way for a few hours, and then your breathing suddenly increases again as your pupils dart back and forth behind your eyelids. This rapid eye movement continues on and off, signifying active brain activity; you're actually dreaming of different ways to take revenge on those cops.

You wake up eight hours later, feeling remarkably refreshed for someone who just slept on concrete after ninety-six hours of abuse and harassment. You stand up, dust yourself off, and continue the walk home that you began a long, long time ago. As you pass along Fifth Avenue, you glimpse the headline of the *New York Post*: SOHO SQUAD SNAGS SOCIALITE SLAYER. You crouch down to take a closer look and shiver when you see the photo of the suspect—he really does look just like you. It's enough to give a person nightmares . . .

six feet under

To awake from what may seem the sweet sleep of returning health, and find one's self not only dressed in the habiliments of the grave, but inclosed [sic] within its remorseless grasp . . . the idea is replete with horror, and the risk should never be permitted.

—*NEW YORK OBSERVER*, 1847

You wake up slowly, blink a few times, and wait for your eyes to adjust to the darkness. Nothing happens. You're not sure where you are or how you got here; the last thing you remember is driving deep into the bayou. But where are you now? You uncross your arms and try to sit up, banging your head on something directly above you. As you rub your bruised scalp, your fingers brush against a rough wooden surface. You try to feel around in the dark but you're barely able to move your arms; your elbows scrape against the rough enclosure. Terror-stricken, you trace the outline of what is confining you. It feels unmistakably like a narrow wooden box—a coffin.

Premature burial is one of our most primal fears, but could it really happen? Sure. For centuries, doctors debated what factors constituted death. Was it enough to simply stop breathing? Have no pulse? No heartbeat? Today, we know that any one of these things does not necessarily mean a person is completely gone. But in the past, doctors weren't quite so sure and in fact developed a number of elaborate tests to determine whether somebody was actually dead. Among the more colorful methods: putting live bugs in a person's ear, pulling their tongue for three days straight, and even administering a tobacco enema (which gives new meaning to the phrase: "Blowin' smoke up your ass").

Even with these "surefire" methods, there are still several anecdotal accounts throughout history of people being buried alive. A nineteenth-century Swedish woman was supposedly buried and later exhumed after a caretaker heard groans from her coffin. Witnesses were aghast to discover that the woman had given birth to a baby. Both were found dead, trapped in their tomb.

And although macabre scholars continue to debate the veracity of these stories, there's no question that the *fear* of being buried alive is definitely real. In nineteenth-century Germany, several "waiting mortuaries" were built where the dead were kept in a room until the onset of putrefaction; these mortuaries were equipped with emergency bells in case any of the corpses awakened. Other inventors (including several Americans) devised coffins that were equipped with similar devices to communicate with the living—just in case.

Even with advancements of modern medicine, there can still be the occasional one that got away. In 1937, a man in France was exhumed by insurance adjusters a few days after a motorcycle accident to ascertain his exact cause of death—and pathologists discovered that he was very much alive and gasping for fresh air. In 1996, a British woman was pronounced dead by a local doctor, but later a policeman saw her foot move and demanded a further inquiry. It turned out the woman was in a diabetic coma.

Now she never made it into a box, but you have. In another era, this might have been an accident—but in your case, it's foul play. You're a vice squad detective in New Orleans and you've been working undercover to infiltrate the operation of a local drug lord. After eighteen months of working to gain their trust, you were finally granted access to their secret drug lab deep in the bayou. Unfortunately, the invitation was just a setup; the bad guys were onto you like flies on roadkill. The last thing you remember is being knocked over the head.

So now what? You pound on the lid and yell, hoping that someone will hear you. But all you do is bruise your fists and use up precious oxygen. You try to angle your body so you can kick at the lid. It's no use—there's barely enough room for you to turn over, let alone swing your leg.

You're basically left in a waiting game. The average adult inhales seven or eight liters, or $\frac{1}{4}$ cubic foot, of oxygen per minute. You're buried in a box with the dimensions of a standard-sized casket: 84 inches long, 28 inches wide, and 23 inches high—a total of 31.3 cubic feet. In other words, you have about two hours in the box before all of the oxygen is depleted.

Your heart is racing a mile a minute and you're sweating. Unfortunately, you're also breathing faster—which depletes the available oxygen and increases the amount of harmful carbon dioxide in the coffin. You rummage through your pockets, trying to find a tool that will help you—but all you appear to be carrying are a book of matches and your housekeys. Then you experience a surge of elation when you reach your inside jacket pocket: those stupid bastards have buried you with your cell phone! You snap it open and punch in the numbers 911. You hear a faint clicking sound but that's it—you don't even get a dial tone. The glowing display screen reads "No Service." Damn that lousy wireless company!

Desperate now, you pound on the lid and scream at the top of your lungs, all too aware that you're wasting oxygen. Then you decide to conserve energy by holding your breath. But this kind of oxygen deprivation only heightens your anxiety and causes you to hyperventilate, which leads to quicker but shorter breaths.

In a last-ditch effort to exhume yourself, you use your keys to scrape at the lid, hoping that you can somehow saw your way out of the box. After an hour of frantic carving, you have made nothing but a small indentation in the lid and a few cuts in your hand. You light a match to survey your work, and then continue lighting all of the matches, one at a time, and watch each one burn down (unaware that you're wasting even more precious oxygen). You manage to calm yourself down by focusing on the glow of the flame. You know you are going to die and you begin to accept it. Minutes slip by. You become very disoriented and sleepy. The amount of oxygen in the coffin is becoming dangerously low.

As the carbon dioxide builds in your lungs and blood, your breathing becomes more labored, and eventually you slip into an unconscious state. You don't feel a thing as the buildup of carbon dioxide quickly leads to respiratory failure and finally brain death. One thing can be said of being trapped alive in a coffin buried six feet under: it's a convenient place to die.

nineteen days in the hole

It seems endless, each morning, behind the same gray door, listening to the same grating noises provoked by steel bruising steel.

—RAY LUC LEVASSEUR, AN INMATE IN SOLITARY CONFINEMENT, COLORADO, 1998

You open your eyes but they might as well be closed. The room is pitch black and you can't see a thing. Your pupils slowly dilate as far as they possibly can—and still you see nothing. You feel around with your hands. The walls are a hard, rough concrete and cool to the touch. The floor is the same. You estimate the dimensions of the tiny space to be around four by six feet—not even enough space to lie down flat. Welcome to your new home.

Solitary confinement is a form of punishment as old as prison itself. In the United States, the use of solitary confinement began in earnest in 1829, as an extension of the Quaker belief that solitude would lead to penitence and reform. Of course, the Quakers didn't consider the irreversible and highly damaging psychological effects. Their methods were pioneered at Philadelphia's Eastern State Penitentiary; when Charles Dickens visited the facility in 1842, he was shocked to discover that many of the inmates were insane. He wrote, "I hold this slow and daily tampering with the mysteries of the brain, to be immeasurably worse than any torture of the body: and because its ghastly signs and tokens are not so palpable to the eye and sense of touch as scars upon the flesh; because its wounds are not upon the surface; and it exhorts few cries that human ears can hear; therefore I denounce it, as a secret punishment which humanity is not roused up to stay."

Despite protests from international visitors and thousands of human rights activists, solitary confinement continues to be used as a form of "rehabilitation" in many American prisons. In 1972 the first "control unit" was opened in Marion Federal Prison in Illinois. In the control unit, inmates are kept isolated from fellow prisoners (and any other human contact) around the clock. New high-tech "super-max" facilities pop up around the country every year, and many are designed to keep inmates in total solitary isolation. (Even the single hour allowed outside the cell for exercise is spent alone.)

You'd give your right arm to be in a super-max facility, where at least inmates have light to read by and occasional television privileges. The year is 1932 and you find yourself imprisoned in Alcatraz, the last stop for the United States' worst offenders. As one of Al Capone's henchmen, you've earned a life sentence behind its walls. The guards are harsh, the cells are cold, and the time is tough. After just two weeks on the island, you hatch a plan to escape, and spend your night chipping away the concrete around a ventilation grate in your cell. One night, while you're quietly toiling away, two guards take an unscheduled tour of the cell and see you. "Hey, what's going on in there, number 14763?"

Before you can even jump back, the guards are upon you. The warden comes by and utters those fateful words: "Take this one to the hole."

The "hole" is a series of isolation cells on Level D of the penitentiary—and its biggest incentive for keeping inmates on their best behavior. As the guards drag you away, the other inmates serenade you with catcalls and rude remarks. You're pushed down a few flights of stairs and then tossed into a tiny room. The large metal door slams behind you with a reverberating thud.

Your thoughts are all you have now. The rest of your senses are totally deprived. No sight. No sounds. Smell? Well, there actually is smell, but you're trying not to think about it. There's no bathroom in this tiny cell—or, then again, the whole thing is a bathroom. Your foot quickly finds a twelve-inch deep hole in the floor and you realize this is what you're supposed to *use*. You're relieved you don't have to go—yet.

A few hours creep by. At least, that's the best that you can figure after slowly counting to sixty about 120 times. You realize that obsessive counting can't be good for your sanity. It's better not to think about the passage of time. You try and lie across the cold floor and get some sleep. But you're too nervous to rest—your heart is racing. When you stand up to pace around the room, you discover that you can only take six small steps in any direction before hitting a wall.

Suddenly, a tiny slot opens in the door, and a beam of light floods across your cell. A guard pushes a plate of bread through the opening, followed by a small tin cup of water. You haven't had a meal in hours, but you just can't bring yourself to eat. Stress is causing compounds called neurotransmitters to be released between the synapses of your brain—and this leads to an incredible amount of anxiety.

An hour later, to your amazement, the large metal door opens. The light flooding in blinds your eyes, as your pupils can't contract fast enough. The guards fling a large object into your cell and then slam the door. "Wait!" you scream after them. "Come back! I need to talk to the warden!" But it's no use. No one is listening, and even if they did hear you, they wouldn't care.

After some groping around in the dark, you realize the guards have given you a mattress to sleep on. But you have no idea if it's morning or night. Is it time to go to bed? You stare into the darkness, trying to estimate the amount of time you've been here, and somewhere along the way you fall asleep.

On the third day, breakfast comes—more bread and water—and you're convinced that you are being poisoned. You know that one guard—the burly one with the big mustache—has had it in for you since you first stepped foot on the Rock. You dump your food in the toilet.

On day five, you hear whispers coming from an adjacent cell. You're elated by the possibility of human interaction—you know that if you could just have a conversation with someone, even for just a few minutes every day, then you'd have no problem keeping it together. But as you listen more closely, you realize that the voice in the adjoining cell belongs to your mother. She's telling someone that you were always an easy child to raise, that you certainly don't deserve to be in a place like Alcatraz.

And this makes no sense, because your mother has been dead for at least ten years. You repeat to yourself over and over: "I'm okay. I'm okay. I'm going to keep it together." But your head is aching and you can't stop scratching your arm. It's almost like a nervous reflex— you're not itching, but your hand goes to scratch it automatically.

Are you going crazy? Not exactly. Psychologists might say that your deprived mind is desperate for attention. The scratching is an attempt to make your body feel any kind of physical stimulation. The paranoid delusions are an attempt to engage your mind in some kind of activity. When the brain is deprived of normal stimulation from natural sur-roundings, it will exhibit a wide range of psychotic behavior.

Dinner. Who knows what day it is. You don't even get up to eat the cold bread. You just stay slumped in the corner. Today, you couldn't even make it to the hole and you soiled yourself. The skin on your forearm is raw and bloody from the constant scratching. You don't know how much longer you can take this.

Days go by and you drift in and out of sleep, unaware of the time of day. Often you wake up and don't know where you are, or even who you are. After nineteen days—the longest possible sentence for soli-tary confinement at Alcatraz—the guards come to set you free. They drag the body of your former self from the hole (you've lost twenty-eight pounds) and the sight of ordinary objects—clocks, shoes, spoons—sends your deprived mind into fits. You are thrown into a shower and hosed off, but you'll never be the same.

You are put in a new cell. There is no ventilation grate. There is no escape.

dancing at the end of your rope

The man hit bottom and I observed that he was fighting by pulling on the straps, wheezing, whistling, trying to get air, that blood was oozing through the black cap . . . I also saw witnesses pass out and have to be carried from the witness room. Some of them threw up.

—CLINTON DUFFY, WARDEN AT SAN QUENTIN FROM 1942 TO 1954,
DESCRIBING HIS FIRST HANGING

As you climb the steps of the gallows, you hear your plastic diaper crinkling underneath your gray jumpsuit, and you hope the corrections officers haven't noticed. It seems completely humiliating to walk to your death dressed in a diaper, but the authorities insisted on it, and a person in your situation has very little bargaining power. A corrections officer slips the noose over your head and tightens it with a swift, hard tug; the initial pressure on your neck is a bit of a reality check.

The warden asks if you would like to make a final statement, and you turn to address the plate-glass window. You can't see the witnesses seated behind it, but you know that they can see you, and that speakers are broadcasting all the sounds from your death chamber. "The state of Delaware is murdering an innocent person tonight," you tell them, which is not exactly true, since you really did shoot a teenage convenience store clerk. But you had only intended to wound the kid—you certainly weren't aiming for his neck. You figure this makes you at least partially innocent, but the district attorney had other thoughts. She's behind the plate-glass window, too, awaiting your demise.

Hanging is one of the world's oldest methods of capital punishment, and it was practiced throughout the United States until the end of the nineteenth century. Way back in the early days, a rope was simply tied into a noose and thrown over an ordinary tree branch; the condemned person was pushed off a cart or stool and slowly strangled to death.

By the late-1800s, however, the British developed a more concise formula for death by hanging: the length of the rope and the distance of the drop were adjusted according to the weight of the prisoner, with the goal of directing exactly 1,260 pounds of force to the neck. The coil of the noose was placed behind the left ear of the condemned person; when the trap door was released, the force would dislocate the third and fourth cervical vertebrae. This effectively tears the spinal cord in two, causing immediate shock and paralysis of respiration. If done properly, the process is thought to be instant and relatively painless.

But getting that perfect drop is almost impossible. More often than not, the length of the rope will be too short (resulting in a painfully slow strangulation) or too long (which results in a gruesome but quick decapitation). After 1890, when firing squads became an accepted practice of capital punishment, most prisoners jumped at the chance to be shot to death. Further innovations led to the electric chair, the gas chamber, and lethal injection, and eventually most states outlawed hanging as cruel and inhumane punishment. But in

Delaware, Washington, and New Hampshire, state-sanctioned hangings are still an option for criminals who have received the death penalty.

You've always had a fear of needles—heck, you tremble at the idea of a tetanus shot—and the idea of lethal injection terrifies you. So you opt for a plain old-fashioned hanging, which actually requires more prep work than you'd expect. The coiled noose is specially formed from Manila hemp that is known for its exceptionally strong fibers. Thirty feet of one-inch-diameter rope is boiled to eliminate the stretch and diminish the tendency to curl. It is formed into six coils and then greased to ensure that the knot will slide easily. After you are weighed, the length of the rope is determined and it is fixed at the top of the gallows.

When you finish speaking your last words, your hands and feet are bound so that there's no way you can stop yourself from falling through the trap. Then an officer slips a black hood over your face, cutting off your view of the world. The prison chaplain steps forward and delivers a quick blessing. Once he's said the word "Amen," you know that your death is imminent, that every extra second is a moment of borrowed time.

And then comes the drop.

It seems like a long time until you feel anything—but you only fall for one-third of a second before the rope is fully extended and the knot constricts around your neck. The force does its intended work, breaking your neck between the third and fourth vertebrae, but your death is not quite instantaneous.

Nerve impulses from the lower half of your body are severed immediately, but you still feel extraordinary pain because nerves in your neck are still communicating with your brain. It is a horrible burst of suffering, but it only lasts a few seconds. *Hypoxia,* or the complete loss of oxygen to the cerebral hemispheres, snuffs out any further feeling.

Spectators should be grateful for the hood, because the face underneath it hardly resembles you anymore. The hypoxia results in a bluish tint to the oxygen-starved tissue, and your skin is also puffy and engorged. Your eyes are protruding and your tongue hangs from your mouth. Below the neck, your heart continues to beat for a few moments, and your arms and legs shudder from spinal reflexes (hence the expression "dancing at the end of your rope"). When your muscles eventually relax, you lose control of your bowels, which explains why the prison insisted that you walk to the gallows dressed in a plastic diaper. Next time, go with the lethal injection.

PART V

EVERYDAY
MISHAPS

express elevator

express elevator ator

I thought we were all going to be killed. It felt like the car was in a free fall. When we hit the bottom, it felt like a crash. We were all huddled together in the corner of the car. I don't know how we got there, but we did. We were in shock.

—GAIL BRODIE, WOMAN WHO ENDURED A SIXTEEN-FLOOR ELEVATOR
FREE FALL IN TORONTO, 2001

As you're locking the door to your office, you hear the familiar chime of an arriving elevator. "Hold the door," you call, and hurry down the hallway. Your actuary firm is on the seventy-ninth floor of New York's Empire State Building, and the wait for an elevator can be excruciatingly long. It's been a hard day of number-crunching and you're anxious to head home. When you reach the elevator, the only other passenger—a bearded businessman in his fifties—is holding the door. "Thanks," you tell him, and step on board.

More than 15,000 people work in the Empire State Building and these employees are transported by seventy-three different elevators. You've been working on the seventy-ninth floor for exactly nine years and seven days. If you get lucky and don't have to make any additional stops, the trip from your office to the lobby should take no more than ninety-seven seconds. (Hey, you're an actuary!)

But a few seconds into your ride, you hear a strange pop from over-head—followed by a metallic snapping that sounds like a buckling piece of sheet metal. The elevator shakes violently and you fall back against the wall, dropping your briefcase. The bearded businessman clutches your arm and releases a bloodcurdling scream. The two of you assume the worst at the same time: you are free-falling the length of the building to the ground below.

There are 600,000 elevators in the United States alone, and millions of people ride them every day, for a total of about 120 billion rides a year. In fact, every three days, around the world, elevators move the equivalent of the earth's entire population. That's a lot of elevator trips, and considering the sheer numbers, an incident like the one you're experiencing is extremely rare. Only about 6,500 people go to the hospital with elevator-related injuries each year, and most of these are due to something like a door closing on a limb, or more minor injures like accidentally tripping while getting off.

What's happening to you is almost unheard of: one of the cables has snapped from wear and tear, causing the elevator to fall unusually fast. The odds of this happening are around one in six million—you're actually thirty times more likely to crack your skull open while get-ting out of bed. Yet despite the stellar safety record of elevators, there are still many people in the world who refuse to ride them; elevator phobia is a diagnosable condition and is often associated with claustrophobia.

The majority of today's elevators employ a pulley, an electric motor, and a counterweight to make the car rise and fall. Known as traction elevators, these machines have anywhere from four to six cables supporting the car—and each alone is strong enough to hold the car's entire weight.

The odds of every elevator cable snapping are astronomically slim—but that did happen in the Empire State Building in 1945, after a small airplane crashed into the famous skyscraper. The impact severed all of the elevator's cables and its lone passenger plummeted seventy-five stories. Her fall was cushioned by compressed air at the bottom of the elevator hoistway, along with a broken cable that had coiled at the bottom of the shaft. Miraculously, the woman survived.

In your case, a secondary cable attached to regulate the speed of the car has snapped. The elevator usually travels around ten feet per second. You are now falling at about twenty feet per second, but that speed is rapidly increasing toward the rate of free fall, which is thirty-two feet per second. Your body senses the increased rate of descent and assumes that you are falling unchecked. The sensation of fear sends you into survival mode and you feel blood drain from your extremities. You're feeling dizzy as your hypothalamus directs increased flow to your brain and muscles, preparing the body for trauma. For the same reason, your breathing becomes deeper and faster.

You want to reach out for the emergency phone but you're afraid to move. Hearing your fellow passenger scream at the top of his lungs doesn't make you any more confident. Your face is pale and your palms are sweating. You know you only have a few moments to act, and you consider trying to jump just as the elevator hits bottom, to lessen the force of impact. But this tactic is almost impossible to time perfectly, and it wouldn't prevent the elevator from collapsing around you (and probably crushing you in mid-jump). A much better plan would be to lie facedown on the floor, in an attempt to distribute the force of impact.

But when the impact finally comes, it's much less deadly than you expect. Your elevator, like almost every elevator in the world, is equipped with a safety braking system. As soon as the car surpassed its usual speeds, a sensor system activated an emergency brake. The car stops suddenly, but your body still carries the momentum of the drop; your legs buckle out from under you and you fall forward onto your knees. Blood immediately begins pooling into the banged-up soft tissue, and your knees will eventually showcase some nasty-looking purple bruises—but for now, these are the worst of your injuries.

Your fellow passenger appears equally unharmed, but he refuses to let go of your arm, and his nonstop blubbering suggests that he'll suffer from elevator phobia for the rest of his life. You pick up the emergency phone and explain your situation to the building supervisor. He quickly confirms your position with his computer—your elevator is hovering just below the twelfth floor—and then he dispatches a crew that will hoist you through the top of the elevator and out of the shaft.

Speaking of the shaft, you feel like you just got it. As you anxiously wait for the rescue crew to arrive, you calculate the amount you plan to sue for: $1,792,000, or roughly a thousand dollars for each floor you plummeted, multiplied by the rate of free fall. For an actuary like yourself, the workday never ends . . .

not-so-lucky strike

not-so-lucky strike

I remember a blinding flash of light and just this inde-
scribable feeling of having something go through my body
and knock me to the ground. I remember coming to just
lying on the ground, disoriented, with no feeling in my
body. For a brief moment, I thought to myself that I might
be dead.

—STEVE ELY, STRUCK BY LIGHTNING IN FLORIDA, 1977

It's Friday afternoon and you've sneaked out of work with a couple
buddies for a quick round of golf. You're just through the front nine of
a Miami country club when the sky grows dark and it starts to drizzle.
Bob suggests packing it in and heading for the clubhouse, but none of
you are very happy with the way you've been playing. Who wants to
end the day with a couple of slices and three balls in the drink?

Feldman points to a small wooden shelter about fifty yards across the fairway. "I think there's a soda machine in there," he says. "Let's make a run for it, and we can wait out the rest of the storm."

Everyone agrees and you set off at a quick pace. You're nearly halfway to the shelter when the clouds really open up, and soon your lime green polo shirt is spattered with big fat raindrops. Then you feel a sudden chill and the hairs on the back of your neck stand up. At that very moment, you hear a loud splitting sound, and then you're surrounded by the brightest light you've ever seen in your life.

Lightning can be an awesome spectacle . . . from a distance. There are approximately two thousand thunderstorms around the earth at any given moment, producing one hundred cloud-to-ground lightning strikes every second. Thanks to its high number of thunderstorms (280 days out of the year), Kampala, Uganda, receives more strikes than any other place in the world. But in the United States, where twenty-six million lightning bolts touch ground annually, the majority will strike in Florida (again, because of the area's high propensity for thunderstorms).

If you happen to be in lightning's way, you will get hurt—very hurt. Imagine the power it takes to run your entire house, then multiply that ten thousand times. That's the kind of power lightning delivers, and the human body—a good conductor of electricity because of its large water content—is not built to withstand that kind of force. The only reason any person hit by lightning is not immediately reduced to ashes is because of the relatively short duration of the contact (even the electric chair needs thirty seconds or more to accomplish its dirty work).

Nevertheless, lightning claims the lives of about one hundred Americans every year, and injures about five hundred more. There are a few simple precautions you can take: Staying indoors is a good idea. So is keeping out of water and avoiding open high ground without trees (like, say, a golf course). But no matter where you are, if you can see lightning, you are at risk for getting the shock of your life.

The flash is blinding and you feel like you're being crushed. It's like a huge weight has been dropped on your shoulders, slamming you into the ground. In fact, a bolt of lightning has entered your body through the right shoulder. One million volts of electricity pass through your body in an instant. The pain is excruciating, but it stops almost as soon as it starts; the last place you feel it is the toe of your right foot. Then you drop to the ground and everything goes black.

When you wake up, the rain has stopped. You're lying on your back in the middle of the fairway. You cannot feel anything below your neck, and you assume you must be dead. Then you hear Bob arguing with Feldman: "If we'd gone back to the clubhouse, we would have been fine." Feldman counters by calling Bob a dumb-ass, and then both of them notice that your eyes are open. "You're going to be all right," Bob assures you. "Just don't move."

Feldman gets on the cell phone with the paramedics and urges them to come faster. "I'm telling you, man," he shouts, "this guy lit up like a lightbulb!" There's a burnt smell in the air and you imagine that your body has been reduced to a pile of ashes. But then you manage to lift your head and see that you're more or less intact—although your right golf shoe is still smoking, your pants are blackened, and your favorite green polo has a gaping, scorched hole in the shoulder.

It could have been a lot worse. Your friends later explain that the bolt of lightning bounced off a tree before striking you in the shoulder; this means you absorbed what is known as a "side splash" rather than the full force of the bolt. As a result, the lightning imparted part of its charge on the tree and you only absorbed a fraction of the electricity it carried to earth—this probably saved your life.

But you are not without your share of injuries. Your head aches and your ears are ringing like you've been sitting in the front row of an AC/DC concert (the sound of the bolt literally blew out the tympanic membrane of your right ear, but it will heal). As the feeling slowly returns to your body, it's accompanied by a searing pain, especially around your shoulder and right foot (these are the areas where lightning entered and exited your body, and they will be clearly marked by third-degree burns and tissue damage deep beneath the skin.)

In its split second of travel through your body, the lightning also wreaked havoc on your cardiovascular and neurological systems. Often, a lightning bolt will stop the heart altogether. Yours received a jolt (not unlike defibrillation) that sent it momentarily into an *arrhythmia*, or irregular heartbeat. Lucky for you, it eventually stabilized. And your nerves, which normally operate by electrical impulses, received an unwanted charge. The permanent damage was slight, although you will be bothered for several months by the "pins-and-needles" sensation in your lower extremities.

You're also sore all over. As the electricity surged through your body, it triggered the muscles to move (just like your nerve impulses would trigger the muscles to move, only much more forcefully and erratically). The results were violent contractions and a series of torn muscles in your chest, shoulders, and abdomen. But these injuries will all heal in time.

The paramedics finally arrive and begin to check your vital stats. You begin to sense that everything will be okay—but as a lightning survivor, you'll still be prey to a number of lingering side effects (many of which doctors and scientists still can't satisfactorily explain). Among them are memory loss (long and short term), sleep disturbance, headaches, loss of dexterity, loss of mathematical skills, irritability, depression, and a loss of hearing. As you lay motionless near that tricky tenth hole, you can't help but wonder how all of this will affect your handicap.

buzzkill kill

Well, when I passed out, my friends put me on the back porch and left me there. A neighbor saw me and called the police and an ambulance. Then I was in the hospital. They pumped my stomach and did some respiratory stuff. I'm not sure exactly what it was, but they did it because when I threw up there was some [vomit] in my lungs.

—TEENAGER JULIE MONAHAN, WHO DRANK THE LION'S SHARE OF A
BOTTLE OF JIM BEAM, 1993

"Woo-hoo! Come on everybody get naked!" You shake your head, exasperated—did somebody really just say that? Under normal circumstances, you're a literary-minded philosophy major who hates when guys act like such overblown clichés. But your holier-than-thou attitude vanishes after you slam a few shots of vodka. Soon you're just

another part of the frat party, jumping around and acting goofy like the rest of the brothers. More drinks are passed your way, and it's clear the party is spiraling out of control. Two half-naked sorority sisters run past you, leading a goat on a leash. But who are you to question a college tradition? Where do you get off being so self-righteous? You uncap a bottle of tequila and take a hearty swig.

Most people understand that alcohol kills, but they figure it'll take years of liver damage before anything bad happens, unless, of course, you drink so much that you get in a car and drive into a tree. These are both common ways for alcohol to kill a person—but even a single night of binge-drinking can be dangerous enough to kill you. In the United States there are more than three hundred reported deaths from alcohol poisoning each year—about as many as deaths attributed to other, "harder" drugs.

Alcohol—ethyl alcohol, specifically—is produced, innocently enough, when airborne yeast combines with water and sugar from a source like potatoes, grains, or fruits. This process, known as fermentation, creates a potent depressive drug that changes brain chemistry. Alcohol reduces and slows the central nervous system and related functions; it can also lead to changes in your moods, feelings, perceptions, and behaviors. In very high doses, alcohol can be as lethal as heroin and cocaine.

The first few drinks make you feel like they always do—they "take the edge off." You're just hanging out with your buds at Sigma Chi, and you start feeling more talkative as the alcohol is ingested. Roughly twenty percent of the alcohol in every drink is absorbed directly into your bloodstream through the walls of your stomach. The rest is absorbed via the small intestine because of its very large surface area. Once in your blood, alcohol needs twenty minutes to circulate to any part of your body where there is water—including major organs like the brain, lungs, kidneys, and heart.

It is your liver's job to dispose of ninety-five percent of the alcohol by converting it to energy. Alcohol can also be excreted through urine, sweat, feces, and breath. (But you already learned about the latter when one of your brothers got too close with his nasty wino breath.)

When it reaches your brain, alcohol makes the skin of your neurons more porous, so that the proper transmission of chemical messages to and from cells becomes disrupted. As you down your sixth or seventh drink, this process is rampant and you start to feel increasingly disoriented. Motor functions begin to slow. You slur your speech. "Give me another shot" is now *"Giff ma ano shootay."* You have clearly not heeded the common warning to avoid more than one alcoholic beverage per hour. It normally takes your liver about two hours to completely oxidize just one drink—and you've had about fifteen. The poor organ simply can't keep up.

Unfortunately, since you're partying at the most popular house on fraternity row, people are ignoring the warning signs that you're in trouble. The half-naked sorority sisters are getting a lot more attention than you. Even that goat is getting more attention. Go figure. You try to tell a brother you're not feeling well, but you're completely incoherent, and he just laughs at you. The room is spinning so fast you can't even see a room; it's like you're staring through a kaleidoscope. You feel your way to a couch and lie down, passing out right in the middle of the party.

But you're not sleeping—you're unconscious. If your friends were paying attention, they might notice your shallow breathing or see that your skin has a slightly purplish hue. The alcohol has slowed several of your most important bodily functions, including heart rate, blood pressure, and breathing rate. As a result, the outer layer of your skin is not receiving enough oxygenated blood. As your body begins to shut down, the people around you are thrashing to the crunching power chords of Limp Bizkit.

Meanwhile, the alcohol is retarding operations in your brain. At this point the infamous "death by choking on your own vomit"—the fate of many a rock star—is a definite possibility. While lying on your back, you could easily throw up and, in effect, be asphyxiated by your own vomit as it falls back into your trachea and blocks the passage of oxygen.

But you won't even make it to this point. With a blood alcohol level of about 0.45 (or roughly four times the legal limit), the concentration of alcohol is so high that the areas of your brain controlling life functions are depressed to the point that they simply stop functioning.

Your brain stops telling your lungs to breathe, and it stops telling your heart to beat.

But the party marches on. When the brothers discover that you're passed out, they assault your body with a black Sharpie marker, scrawling words like "Poser" and "Lightweight" on your face and neck. Then they construct a massive pyramid of pizza boxes and empty beer cans over your body. Everybody thinks it's hilarious now, but they won't be laughing in the morning.

acid test

In the movie *Alien*, there's a scene where crew members are startled to see a fist-sized hole in their spaceship's ceiling, still sizzling from some substance that has just burned clear through the metal. I have met the closest thing there is to that alien's blood. It came in a small plastic bottle, and it was eating its way through my patient's hand.

—DR. JEREMY BROWN, ON THE EFFECTS OF HYDROFLUORIC
ACID, 1996

It's the middle of the night when you're awakened by a twinge of pain in your right hand. The fingers seem to burn a bit, but you dismiss the sensation as part of a dream. You roll over and try to fall back to sleep, but the pain steadily increases, and finally you get up and walk to the bathroom. You flip on the light and examine your hand to see if there's anything visibly wrong. It looks fine—no bleeding, no swelling, not even a little redness.

But the pain is becoming much worse, like there's a fire burning in your fingers. You hold your hand under cold water, but even this doesn't bring any kind of relief. What could it be? Your sleepy mind reflects on all of your actions from the previous day and finally zeroes in on the hour you spent cleaning your new Camaro. You remember using an industrial-strength solvent to scrape a little tar off your shiny chrome wheels—could that have anything to do with the pain you're feeling right now? You phone your local hospital to find out.

Acid is your problem, a chemical compound that can be deadly. Countless Chemistry 101 textbooks have defined acid as "any compound that can transfer a proton to any other compound." But this kind of definition doesn't even hint at acid's incredible potential for destruction. The sulfuric acid in your Camaro's car battery, for example, could eat right through the hood of the vehicle.

As you listen to the emergency room's on-hold music, you think back to your work in the garage. You remember feeling horrified by the sight of black tar on your otherwise spotless wheels. You quickly rummaged through a cardboard box full of cleaning supplies and discovered an old bottle labeled, appropriately enough, "Tar Remover." The directions advised you to wear protection when using the product, so you grabbed a pair of latex gloves from under the kitchen sink. Then you found yourself a good rag and went to work.

What you didn't realize was that the tar remover contained *hydrofluoric acid* (HF), one of the strongest of all inorganic acids—in fact, exposure to a single droplet of HF can cause hours of excruciating pain. In the United States, more than a thousand cases of HF exposure are reported every year—often thanks to poorly labeled cleaning products like your tar remover. A more accurate warning label might read: "Absolutely under no circumstances should this product ever make even the *slightest* contact with your skin, period."

To make matters worse, your latex gloves had a few small holes that you didn't notice. As you splashed the tar remover onto the rag, a small amount leaked through the glove and seeped onto your fingers and palm. While you scrubbed away at the chrome, you felt nothing—except the elation of seeing your wheels looking shiny once again. You disposed of the rag and gloves, went inside your house, and thoroughly washed your hands with soap and water—a job well done. But as the evening progressed, something horribly sinister was happening inside your hand.

Unlike other acids, hydrofluoric acid doesn't damage the surface of the skin; instead, it rapidly penetrates the epidermis and is absorbed by deeper tissue. Since hydrofluoric acid doesn't carry a charge, its molecules can easily slip through the fatty surfaces of membranes. Hydrogen and fluoride ions quickly pass through the *stratum corneum*, a tough, waterproof layer of dead cells, and eventually reach living cells that are deep inside your hand.

The fluoride ion attacks these living cells and causes what is known as *liquefaction necrosis* of the tissue: the watery breakup of cells. The hydrogen ion binds with the calcium in the soft tissue to aid and expedite this destruction. Because the process disrupts the body's electrolyte balance, it can lead to abnormal heart rhythms, circulatory collapse, and eventually even death.

Your contact with the acid is nowhere near life-threatening but still extremely painful. Your newly deceased cells release potassium, which greatly irritates the many surrounding nerve endings. Those nerves relay their irritation to the brain, which eventually causes you to awaken in the middle of the night. By the time you speak with someone at the emergency room, you're speaking incoherently, babbling about your Camaro and a burning sensation in your hand. It takes awhile, but eventually you mutter the two magic words: tar remover. The nurse advises you to get to the hospital immediately. Fortunately, it's just a few short miles away, because you're driving in a pain-induced haze and can barely concentrate on the road.

At the hospital, a group of emergency room doctors debate the best possible way to treat your condition (it's not a very comforting spectacle). Finally, one of the nurses suggests calling the local poison control center to determine the proper treatment. You've been awake for more than an hour now and the pain is becoming unbearable; thousands of cells are dying inside you, and you would gladly consider amputation if it guaranteed the pain would stop.

Then the door to your examination room opens. Salvation has arrived in the form of a medical resident dressed in green OR scrubs; she uncaps a small plastic tube and gestures for you to put out your hand. "You'll thank me in a minute," she tells you, before liberally applying the ointment to your fingers and palm.

The active ingredient in the ointment is *calcium gluconate*, a solution that neutralizes the acid by replacing the calcium that the acid has stripped from your tissue. With the gel on your hand, the pain lessens almost immediately, and after just a few minutes, the burning has completely stopped. Now with a clearer head and the knowledge that you will completely recover, you're beginning to wish you'd just left the tar on your wheels.

No, wait, what are you thinking? That's your Camaro!

blow-dryer in the bathtub

Our best guess is that there are millions of hair dryers still in use that don't provide any protection from electrocution in water.

—RICK FROST, U.S. CONSUMER PRODUCT SAFETY COMMISSION, 1997

It's barely noon and your office has already called three times. First the computers were down. Then they couldn't find the fourth quarter projections. And then they called because the photocopier was jammed! What's next? They're out of coffee stirrers?

Your plan was to stay home, watch a little television, and take a breather from a recent stretch of twelve-hour workdays (you manage a busy telemarketing firm that makes thousands of phone calls every day, and a recent long-distance promotion has left you totally frazzled).

Since nothing relaxes you faster than a nice long bath, you begin filling the tub with water. You also set your cordless on the bathroom sink, because you're certain that some bozo from the office will call with another stupid question.

As you ease yourself into the steaming water, you feel the tension melt away—until, sure enough, the phone rings. As you reach up for the cordless, your elbow brushes against a long coiled cord that ascends from a wall outlet and ends in a blow-dryer that's perched high on a shelf. This collision provides just enough force to unsettle the appliance from its perch, and the blow-dryer begins to fall. Your mouth hangs open and your body stiffens as the appliance splashes into the water.

With its wet, slippery floors, scalding hot water, and an array of electrical grooming devices, the bathroom can be a real danger zone. In a typical year, the U.S. Consumer Product Safety Commission reports some 71,000 injuries in and around the bath and shower, and around 360 accidental deaths. Being electrocuted after accidentally dropping the blow-dryer in a full tub of water is more than a cinematic way to die—it's a very real danger. Until 1991, there were almost twenty such deaths reported every year. It was about that time that the small appliance industry began installing ground-fault circuit interrupters (GFCI) in all new hair dryers.

With a GFCI, a hair dryer will automatically block the flow of current once there is an imbalance in the electrical signal (like when a plugged-in hair dryer is dropped into a tub full of water). Unfortunately, there are still millions of older hair dryers in use without GFCIs. In fact, adding the protection is nothing more than a voluntary industry standard, and many manufacturers continue to make new hair dryers without the device (especially abroad). As soon as the Consumer Product Safety Commission gets wind of such an appliance, there's a product recall, but that doesn't mean you can't have one hiding in your closet.

You don't even remember what bargain bin you pulled your hair dryer out of. All you knew was that it was nice and small, perfect for travel, and very cheap. Unfortunately, the few extra dollars you saved on your dryer are about to finance your early demise. As the blow-dryer hits the water, the current from the wall immediately creates a voltage field in the tub. Your foot kicks against the metal faucet, completing the circuit, and the current goes straight through your body. Because the human body is sixty percent water, it happens to be a very good conductor of electricity—and when soaked in a bathtub of water, it's even better.

It would have helped if your hair dryer had a GFCI (in which case you would trip the circuit with nary a shock). The bathroom outlets of many newer homes are also equipped with GFCIs, but there's no chance to ask your landlord about it now.

The last thing you feel are a few milliseconds of dread as the blow-dryer slips off the shelf—and then 110 volts begin streaking through your body. Your muscles spasm wildly from the electricity, which interrupts normal nerve function. You can't breathe as your diaphragm (also a muscle) is paralyzed by the shock. But worst of all, your heart goes into immediate fibrillation, and the wild beating does not allow enough blood to reach your brain. You lose consciousness before you can even curse whoever's on the other end of that phone.

You die roughly ten seconds after the hair dryer hits the water—and that's just enough time for your answering machine to click on, greet the caller, and invite her to leave a message. She does: "Good afternoon. My name is Cheryl and I'm calling to tell you about an exciting new long-distance program. Did you know that you could be saving fifty percent, sixty percent, even seventy-five percent on your telephone bills?"

it's just gas

It feels like somebody's stabbing me in the head. We can't move—we're paralyzed.

—LISA DICKERSON, A PENNSYLVANIA WOMAN DESCRIBING THE
EFFECTS OF CARBON MONOXIDE POISONING, 1998

You feel a mild headache coming on so you decide to just hit the sack. It must be the holiday season—too much time with your folks always gives you a headache. You've just returned from a long Christmas dinner where your mother nagged you for not being married and not giving her grandkids and not pursuing a more lucrative profession. You were barely finished with your plum pudding when you hurried out the door—and then drove two hours back to your country cottage, just to get a little peace and quiet.

It's a chilly night, so you crank up your new kerosene heater and climb into bed, wrapping yourself in a down comforter. By morning your headache is a lot worse; the intensity of the pain wakes you up from a restless sleep. You also feel vaguely nauseated. It's almost like you have the world's worst hangover—but you haven't been drinking.

You decide it's best to just stay in bed. You're completely exhausted and feel like you haven't slept all night. You slump your head back and close your eyes, trying to fight the increasing nausea. You take deep breaths and wonder what your mother served that could make you feel this way. Spoiled ham? Bad eggnog? Maybe it's the flu? Just about everyone in your family has had a touch of the flu this winter, so you figure it's your turn. But how could it strike so quickly?

By the end of the day, you'll wish you just had the flu. You're actually dealing with a deadly enemy known as carbon monoxide, an odorless, colorless compound that is extremely poisonous to human beings and yet ubiquitous in our society. CO is the by-product of fuel combustion, and it is produced by furnaces, stoves, fireplaces, clothes dryers, automobiles, and, yes, kerosene space heaters. If any one of these appliances should happen to malfunction, watch out.

Carbon monoxide is the leading cause of accidental poisoning in the United States. Around 1,500 Americans die every year from inadvertent exposure to CO in the home. (Unfortunately, another 2,300 die from *intentional* exposure—closing the garage door and starting the car is a popular way to do yourself in.) But if you recognize the warning signs—headache, dizziness, fatigue—it's possible to survive; more than 10,000 people are treated successfully every year for accidental exposure to CO. But in order to get help, they had to get themselves away from the gas.

You can't even get out of bed. The dangers of your malfunctioning space heater are heightened by the relatively small size of your cabin; with no open windows or doors, it doesn't take long before most of the air is tainted with carbon monoxide. Now the deadly gas is slowly wreaking havoc on your respiratory and circulatory systems.

When you breathe fresh air under normal circumstances, the oxygen binds with a molecule called hemoglobin, which is found in your red blood cells. It's hemoglobin's job to transport the oxygen from your lungs to various parts of your body. When the oxygen/hemoglobin complex reaches a muscle where it is needed, the oxygen is then released. Hemoglobin is used over and over again to pick up oxygen and move it throughout the body.

But the carbon monoxide in your cabin is interfering with this all-important transport system. With every breath you take, a little CO follows the oxygen down your trachea; upon arriving in your lungs, it competes with the oxygen to bind with the hemoglobin molecule.

And here's the kicker: In a cruel biological irony, most of the hemo-globin in your blood actually *prefers* the carbon monoxide and holds on to it even more tightly than oxygen. The new compound that is formed is called *carboxyhemoglobin*.

As you breathe the carbon monoxide–contaminated air, more and more oxygen transportation sites on the hemoglobin molecules become blocked by carboxyhemoglobin. Gradually, there are fewer and fewer sites available for oxygen. Without enough oxygen, cellu-lar metabolism is disrupted, and eventually cells begin to die, espe-cially those in your heart and brain.

At this point, you can't even make a phone call to get help. You have lost all of your motor skills. The tissues of your body are liter-ally starving for oxygen. Your heart rate accelerates, your eyes close, and you lose consciousness. The dying cells of the heart cause a dis-turbance in rhythmic beating. Your ventricles are not filling properly with blood and the circulation to your brain is diminished. Within moments after your brain stops functioning, you are dead.

The next day, your mother drives to your home bearing an apology and a fruitcake. When she enters your home, she finds you lying very still in your bed, and looking surprisingly healthier than you looked the night before. Carboxyhemogoblin makes your blood brighter and more vibrant than normal, so you actually have the complexion of an Olympic athlete after a particularly vigorous match.

But your mother is not comforted. She drops the fruitcake and runs out of the house screaming.

PART VI

GOING TO EXTREMES

bent out of shape
bent out of shapehape

Every part of my body hurt. My insides felt as if they were being forcibly rearranged.

> —DIVER BERNIE CHOWDHURY, WHO SUFFERED THE BENDS WHILE DIVING AT THE WRECK OF THE *ANDREA DORIA*, 1991

After a quick last-minute check of your air tank, your regulator, and, of course, your trusty dive computer, you suit up and jump flipper-first into the choppy water. Your crew is exploring the remains of a sunken whaling ship at the bottom of the Atlantic Ocean; to reach it, you descend nearly 150 feet below sea level.

By the light of your dive lamp, you swim through the dark, murky depths and explore the wreckage. While crossing over the deck, you notice a large crack in the ship's hull, and you swim through it in search of hidden artifacts: a coin, a pitcher, some silverware, anything that might help pay for this diving expedition (or at least get you on *Antiques Roadshow*).

But you don't find a thing. You're obviously not the first group to scavenge the remains of this boat, and its contents have been stripped clean. The other members of your team give you the thumbs-down sign, and indicate that they'll be swimming back up to the surface. You wave them off, deciding to spend a little more time enjoying the scenery. You're in no hurry to return to the surface, where the staggering bills for this failed expedition will be waiting for you.

After nearly an hour underwater, your dive computer signals it is time to begin a slow ascent to the surface. You adjust your buoyancy control device to aid your climb, and then glance back at the digital screen to determine your first decompression stop. Suddenly, you're seized by fear. The screen is blank! The dive computer—which cost more than two thousand dollars and came with a lifetime guarantee—must be malfunctioning. It contains the information you need to plan the most important part of your dive, the rate of ascent. Without this information, there's a very strong risk that you could rise to the surface too quickly. Your panic increases and you breathe faster through your respirator, increasing the level of carbon dioxide in your system and wasting more of the precious air left in your tank. You're going to have to wing it—you just pray that you don't get the bends.

The bends is an enigma that kills you from the inside out. The air in your tank (like the air you breathe every day) is composed of twenty percent oxygen and eighty percent nitrogen. While you inhale, this nitrogen is absorbed by tissues throughout your body. But as you dive deeper and deeper, this nitrogen becomes very compressed—and more and more of it is absorbed by your body's tissues. When you attempt to resurface, you need to proceed very slowly, pausing to stop at least once, so the compressed nitrogen will have enough time to exit your body. Otherwise, it will begin decompressing all at once—and it will literally bubble up inside your tissues, interrupting the flow of blood. If this happens, you face serious injury or even death.

This affliction was common among laborers constructing the Brooklyn Bridge in the 1870s. After descending to the bottom of the East River in huge pressurized enclosures, they would surface with horrible pains. Many were doubled over in agony—and their posture was similar to a fashionable high-society walk known as the Grecian bend. The bridge-builders abbreviated the condition to simply "the bends."

In the United States alone, there are more than three million recreational divers, and every last one of them is aware of the risks (thanks in large part to dive training and the mandatory classes that every prospective diver must take). Many people mistakenly believe that you have to be a serious diver to get the bends—but this condition can strike divers of any skill level who travel more than thirty-three feet below sea level. To prevent decompression sickness, most people rely on a strict dive table that was devised by scientists in the beginning of the twentieth century. The table informs divers of safe depths and the proper rate of ascent necessary for dissolved gases to safely exit the body.

All of this very vital information was stored on your dive computer, so now you're going to have to wing it. Since you've done a fair amount of diving, you could probably make an educated guess about decompression time—if you were thinking clearly. But that's a pretty big *if*. Right now, you feel like you've just done a few shots of tequila. This is the result of another diver's malady—known as *nitrogen narcosis*—where nitrogen is forced under pressure to your bloodstream and eventually your brain, where it distorts electromagnetic signals and makes you feel as if you've been drinking.

Like a drunk, you have a slightly euphoric feeling and a false confidence. You slowly ascend to about fifty feet and wait for your body to properly decompress. You try counting off seconds to time yourself, but keep losing track. The nitrogen narcosis is preventing you from thinking clearly. Only ten minutes or so pass, but to you, it feels more like thirty—and that's enough time for you to resume your ascent to the surface.

As you near the bottom of the expedition boat, the nitrogen narcosis fades and you begin to doubt your calculations. Did I wait long enough? Did I surface too fast? You break the surface, bracing yourself for the worst, but you still feel fine. You wave to the rest of your crew and begin swimming to the boat. So far, so good. You decide that—as soon as you get back to dry land—you're going to take your defective diving computer back to the salesman and raise some serious hell.

But halfway up the ladder to your boat, a savage pain grips your chest. You scramble onto the deck and you can barely breathe; all you can do is signal to your equipment, to try to indicate you have some sort of problem. "Oh, he's bent real bad," says the first mate.

Due to the sudden change in pressure, inert nitrogen gases are now bubbling out of your body's tissues and blocking the flow of your blood. Your lungs feel like you've swallowed scalding hot coffee. You collapse on the deck of the boat, unable to move because nitrogen has obstructed the blood vessels around your spinal cord. Adding to your agony are severe nausea, increased difficulty breathing, and blurred vision.

This is as bad as decompression sickness gets—and you know that your chance of survival is almost nil. If you're lucky, you may "walk away" with permanent paralysis or (since blood is being blocked from your brain) a near-fatal stroke. But the pain is so severe that you would gladly choose death rather than endure the feeling for much longer. It feels like a thousand creatures are trying to claw their way out of your body.

As you writhe in agony, your crew has signaled for help. Your only real (albeit slim) chance for survival is immediate placement in a recompression chamber, which is designed to lower the pressure and reacclimate your body. Lucky for you, there's a Coast Guard base nearby, and they dispatch a chopper that whisks you to a naval hospital in less than an hour.

An hour later, you're semiconscious and lying in a fifteen-foot-long iron tank with two-inch-thick walls. You're breathing pure oxygen through a mask, and the tank has been pressurized to simulate an environment 150 feet below sea level. As the nitrogen gas slowly escapes from the tissues of your body, the pain begins to subside. Doctors decrease the pressure gradually, over the course of six hours, until its atmosphere has returned to normal. Miraculously, you will make a full recovery.

But if you thought a diving expedition was expensive, just wait until you get the bill for six hours in a recompression chamber. Too bad you didn't find any artifacts to pay for it . . .

barrel o' laughs

Oh God, it hit hard.

—JOHN DAVID MUNDAY, ON GOING OVER NIAGARA FALLS IN A
BARREL, 1993

The barrel-shaped container is six feet tall and made of reinforced steel. It weighs six hundred pounds, but to keep it upright in the water, you've filled it with another two hundred pounds of sand. The inside is lined with heavy foam padding, and there's probably enough room for two normal-sized adults to squeeze inside. Of course, you're the only person you know who's crazy enough to try this stunt—so you'll have plenty of room to stretch out.

Your crew strikes at dawn, just before the tourists begin to arrive. You drive up to a small tree-lined area on the Canadian side of the falls, just a few hundred feet upstream from the tourist observation decks.

Everyone works quickly and quietly, aware that the Niagara police do not exactly condone daredevil stunts. (If you're caught anywhere near the water with anything resembling a barrel, you're likely to face a steep fine or even imprisonment.) You climb into the barrel, don your crash helmet, and give the thumbs-up sign to your crew. Then they fasten the waterproof lid, shutting out the morning light.

It seems like an odd combination: a massive waterfall and a big ol' barrel. But the two have been curiously linked for over a hundred years. Ever since 1886, when English barrel-maker Carlisle D. Graham staged a stunt where he bobbed around in the rapids below the falls, daredevils have been using barrels to navigate the famous natural wonder. The first person to actually go over in a barrel was Michigan schoolteacher Annie Taylor, who took the plunge in 1901. She survived, but once liberated from her four-and-a-half-foot-long barrel, Taylor managed to say—to anyone who would listen—"Nobody ought ever do that again."

Not everybody has heeded Annie's warning. A number of thrill-seekers have followed the schoolteacher's lead—some successfully, some not. Since Crazy Annie went down, fourteen others have tried it, but only nine lived to tell their tale. The question is: Will you?

Here's what you're up against: The famous Horseshoe Falls is 173 feet high and every second, 600,000 gallons of water pour over the width of its 2,500-foot-long crest line. Every minute, more than three hundred million pounds of water pass over the falls, and the force of this water is so great it can actually carve rock. (In fact, thanks to the ceaseless pounding of the water, scientists estimate the site of the falls has moved seven miles since its creation 12,000 years ago.) It should come as no surprise that utility companies eventually tried to harness this incredible force—and nowadays, the falls is the largest producer of electric power in the world.

Tourists travel from around the world to view Niagara Falls from the safety of sturdy observation decks. You, on the other hand, will come much closer than any sane person would want to. It's pitch black in your homemade contraption, and the darkness only adds to your rising feeling of dread. You can no longer hear the voices of your friends, but you know they must be panting and grunting as they push the heavy barrel toward the bank of the river. Then suddenly your vessel pitches sideways, and you feel yourself bobbing on the surface of the water. Time to take a few deep breaths. You're only six hundred yards from the edge of the falls—about one minute away from the main event. In response to your growing anxiety, the brain signals your adrenal glands to secrete adrenaline, and your heartbeat begins to accelerate.

You slowly count down from sixty, trying to anticipate the exact moment you'll go over. But then the current accelerates and the roar of the falls becomes deafening; even your insulated barrel and crash helmet can't block out the sound. You stop counting and just brace yourself, by curling your knees to your chest and tucking your head in a fetal position. You're not even sure if this will help to protect you, but it seems to make you feel better.

Suddenly, it feels like the bottom has dropped out, and you're floating in the air. For a moment, it's pleasant—but just for a moment. Then you crash hard into a rocky outcropping and your barrel is flipped upside down. You crash a second time and your body slams into the side of your steel cocoon. As the barrel continues to tumble, you slam again and again, trying to brace yourself with your hands, but you have no idea where the force will send you next. When you were preparing for this stunt, you never entertained the possibility that you might die. Now, as you're being whipped around like a pinball, you understand with startling certainty that you are not going to make it.

Your descent from the top of the falls lasts only four seconds—but it feels much longer. When you hit bottom, the force sends you straight up against the lid of your barrel. Your "crash helmet" lives up to its name, and smashes into the metal top of the barrel with a bone-crushing force. Inside your head, your brain smacks against the side of your skull—and the resulting trauma causes a momentary disruption in the chemical connections between brain cells. You fall unconscious.

Meanwhile, your barrel is being pummeled by the cascading falls—you splash down underwater before the buoyancy bounces you back to the surface, and the flow of the rushing water leads you away from the falls. Your ground crew runs along the base of the river, following your progress and doing its best to quickly haul you to shore.

You wake up a few minutes later, feeling very sore and very groggy. Your body aches from crashing into the sides of your barrel; at each point of impact, blood from tiny broken vessels has escaped into the surrounding subcutaneous tissues, which means that you're going to have some pretty gigantic black-and-blue spots. But you're alive.

Now your only concern is getting out of the damn barrel. It's dark, claustrophobic, and (most importantly) only has a limited supply of oxygen. Fortunately, your pals on shore manage to get a rope around the barrel and haul you to shore. When they pry open the lid, you're still too weak to pull yourself out. But as the sun casts a warm glow on your face, you manage a feeble smile, knowing that you've survived what only a handful of idiots have managed before. Congratulations.

major league pain pain

I knew I was hurt bad, but I was talking and my sight was okay. I was in shock. I wanted to know what happened.

—TEXAS RANGERS' CATCHER DON SLAUGHT, HIT BY A PITCH AT
BOSTON'S FENWAY PARK, 1986

When the PA announcer says your name, forty thousand fans rise to their feet, cheering like mad and chanting your name. As you stride to home plate, you realize this is the storybook moment you've dreamed about since you were a kid: it's the bottom of the ninth, your team is down by three, and the bases are loaded. You dig your cleats into the soft red dirt, take a few practice swings, and glare out at the opposing pitcher. He's looking back at his catcher and shakes off a sign before beginning his windup. You quickly run through the possibilities; this guy usually throws a first-pitch fastball to set up the curve, but since he just shook off the sign, you're pretty sure it's going to be the hook. You watch him wind up and carefully study his hand, waiting to pick up the ball as he releases it.

A typical major league pitch travels sixty feet, six inches—the distance between home plate and the pitcher's mound—in about four-tenths of a second. You have less than half that time to decide if you want to begin your swing. You see the ball coming in high and inside, but you're guessing it's a breaking ball and believe the pitch will curve out over the plate. In the last tenth of a second before the ball is upon you, you see that it's coming in fast and not breaking—it's the heater. You abort your swing and drop your hands in an effort to turn away from the projectile—a 5¼-ounce sphere with a cork-and-rubber center wrapped in 219 yards of wool yarn, 150 yards of cotton string, and topped with a cowhide cover. *Thwack!* You hear a terrible sound, and then everything goes black.

With its languid pace and beautifully manicured playing fields, baseball seems as safe as a walk in the park—especially when compared to the crunching force of football and the death-defying, midair acrobatics of basketball. Nevertheless, almost 500,000 baseball-related injuries are treated in hospitals each year. In fact, you can actually die playing the game (young children with limited skills have the highest risk). But these facts should come as no surprise in a game where balls are hit and thrown as hard as humanly possible.

According to the U.S. Consumer Product Safety Commission, eighty-eight children died playing baseball between 1973 and 1995. Sixty-eight of these deaths were caused by a simple blow to the chest. If the ball strikes you in just the right spot—during the tenth of a second in which your heart is preparing to beat—a powerful shock wave can be sent into the organ, jolting it into an arrhythmia and resulting in a heart attack.

Or consider the two outfielders in the Babe Ruth League (Little League for sixteen to eighteen year olds) who collided in a 2001 game while going after a fly ball. The center fielder suffered a fracture to his larynx and *cricoid*, the cartilage around the larynx; as a result, he suffocated and died. This may sound like just another freak accident—but bean-balls are definitely not. Getting hit by a pitched ball—sometimes intentionally—is part of the game, and often leaves Major League baseball players with both emotional and physical scars.

You've suffered the worst kind of injury—a fast ball right to the face. The impact jars your brain and causes a momentary disturbance in the organ's electrical activity, which results in a blackout. You awaken on the ground a few moments later, knowing full well what happened, but not sure if your head is still in one piece. You reach for your face and feel a lot of fresh blood. Your entire face stings with pain, and you can't tell where the hurt is coming from. Your eye? Your cheek? Who knows? "Oh, geez!" yells the catcher, which does not make you feel better about the extent of your injuries. "Oh, geez! Somebody get a stretcher!" You are conscious but very woozy.

Your accident was serious enough to bring a stadium of 40,000 rabid fans to a hush. A baseball traveling at ninety-five miles per hour has struck you pretty squarely in the right eye. The force of the ball has split the skin around the eye and ruptured blood vessels just under the skin, leaving your face very bloody. But even worse is that the ball has broken the small orbital bone below your eye, causing what's known as an *orbital blowout fracture*.

Your eye socket is a bony cup that protects the eye, with a thick layer of bone around the rim and a very thin layer beneath the eye, which is known as the floor. The pressure created by the force of the ball on your eye socket ruptures the floor. Part of this bone is now pushing into the ocular muscles, limiting movement of your eye.

To top it off, the ball grazed the eyeball itself, and caused a hemorrhage into the anterior chamber of the eye. This makes it look very red and bloody, but will not cause any lasting, long-term damage. The tissue surrounding your eye was also damaged, and the blood streaming from broken vessels creates the classic black-eye look.

As one might expect, you are feeling a considerable amount of pain. The nerves in the broken bones are firing, as well as the nerves in the split tissue surrounding the eye. And whenever you look around to try to assess your injuries, your ocular muscles scrape against fractured bits of bone, triggering pain deep within the eye socket.

But it could be worse. The damage to your eye has not affected the retina or the optic nerve (hooray for evolution—the physical location of your eye, tucked deep in its socket, helps prevent most injury from blunt trauma). Surgery saves your vision while ESPN *SportsCenter* shows the clip of you getting clocked ad infinitum. And on top of all that, your team actually wins the game. The pitcher is so shaken up that he lays a fat pitch down the middle of the plate; your teammate—a rookie—hits the game-winning homerun and goes on to a career as a Hall of Famer. You have to settle for hundreds of get-well cards from adoring fans. All things considered, it could have been a lot worse.

nine rounds of heavyweight boxing

I wanted to drive that bone up into his brain.

—MIKE TYSON, ON BOXER JESSE FERGUSON'S NOSE, 1986

You stagger. A mixture of sweat and blood stings your eyes and obscures your vision. Your legs feel like heavy lead pipes, barely responding under your hulking 215-pound frame. You keep your guard up, circle around the ring, and wait for another moment to strike. You muster just enough energy for two quick jabs to his body, but they barely graze the sturdy abdomen. You move back, watch his hands, and wait.

He lunges forward. A punch strikes your chest like a battering ram. At first you're just numb—but then the pain rises from your gut and permeates your upper body. Even your insides seem to hurt. Your hands drop down for only a second, but in that instant two more blows hit your face—one to your already-split chin and the second to your right temple. It feels like your head is knocked off your body. The force of the punches knocks you off your feet and you fall, watching the canvas come closer and closer until you land with a heavy thud and bounce. You are almost relieved. Being down on the mat will afford you some solace, a peaceful moment of quiet time where no one will be punching your head.

As a sport, boxing can be attached to just about every superlative: oldest, most primal, most inherently violent, most painful, most dangerous. It is also the most basic of games: Two people stand in a square and have a certain amount of time to punch each other silly. There is evidence of boxing in ancient Greece and Mesopotamia, as far back as 1500 B.C., and fist-fighting was even an Olympic sport in 668 B.C. The Romans made things a bit more interesting by giving metal-spiked gloves to the combatants. Boxing died out during the Middle Ages when religious doctrine prohibited using the body for physical play, but was revived in Great Britain in the eighteenth century.

In 1867, the Marquis of Queensberry at Cambridge University developed the rules of boxing that have remained unchanged to this day. Boxers used padded gloves and fought ten three-minute rounds with a one-minute break in between. A fighter who was knocked down had ten seconds to stand up or else would lose the match. The Marquis also divided combatants by weight class and introduced the point-scoring system.

Today, there are myriad belts and divisions and championships, but boxing is basically unchanged. And it's still an extremely brutal sport. An estimated fifty boxers have died in the past thirty years. A punch from a heavyweight boxer can carry a crushing force of up to ten thousand pounds—the equivalent force of a bat hitting a baseball. That kind of power results in countless injuries, including (but not limited to) bloody noses, broken noses, perforated ear drums, swollen lips, bruised ribs, concussions, broken hands, broken ribs, broken jaws, and broken cheekbones.

As a heavyweight boxer, you're well aware of the risks and the pain. You've spent months preparing for this fight, and as you make your way from the trainer's room to the ballroom of Caesar's Palace, you can think of nothing but knocking your opponent's head off. The blood-thirsty crowd is cheering like mad—but most of them appear to be rooting for the champ, not you. Doesn't matter, though—as soon as you step foot in that ring, you get into your zone. You're oblivious to the crowd, the cameras, the sexy ring card girls, and even the ref (who's currently urging you both to have a "good, clean fight").

The pituitary gland at the base of your brain is already producing generous amounts of endorphins. These chemicals will bind to nerve receptor sites in your brain and act as a natural painkiller; they also make you feel focused and electrified. When the first bell rings, you emerge from your corner slowly, sizing up your gigantic opponent. His eyes are cold black pools, showing no emotion. His first two blows strike your solar plexus, temporarily interrupting the signal sent by your phrenic nerve (this basically disables your diaphragm and renders you unable to breathe—but only for a moment). You lumber backward, anxious to land a punch of your own. But the champ deftly blocks your advance and your glove barely grazes his arm.

Even in the first round, the limits of your physical endurance are already being tested. You breathe hard to feed your muscles, which are using copious amounts of oxygen to function at peak levels. There are a lot of punches thrown, but no good connects on either side. The round ends and you retreat to your corner, where your trainer is furious. "What are you doing out there?" he asks. "Move and punch. Move and punch. Don't ever drop your guard!" Even though he's screaming in your ear and literally spitting in your face, he might as well be down the Strip at Bally's. You're in a zone, just breathing, tuning out Doc, tuning out the cheers, and thinking about getting back out there.

The second bell rings and you decide to come out swinging. You offer a quick combination to the head and you make good contact on the southpaw, but you feel like the champ is laughing at you, just daring you to punch. You go in for the kill and you're blocked. And then it comes—the first clean punch landed by the champion to your face. Fortunately, you're wearing a mouth guard that prevents any of your teeth from becoming dislodged (it also reduces the risk of concussion and protects your lower jaw from snapping off the base of your skull).

But your bottom lip splits, and blood supplied by your facial artery starts streaming down your chin.

This taste of blood fires you up for the rest of the round, and you land a flurry of jabs, backing your opponent up against the ropes. "Hey, hey, break it up!" implores the referee, who physically separates you from your opponent.

The third round is a tough one. You're getting tired and you're starting to lose your balance. As you stumble, a punch lands on your right eye, rupturing the dermis tissue above the socket. The vessels burst and blood spills over your face. When you regain your balance, the champ lands another punch to your ribs, and you hear the snap of splintering bone. This round cannot end soon enough.

In your corner, you're attended to by your "cut man," who shoves a large Q-Tip soaked in adrenaline chloride into the open wound. It quickly shrinks the leaking blood vessels. He further closes the wound with a dab of Vaseline. You take a swig of water but it's hardly what you'd call refreshing.

The next few rounds are a grind. Your muscles are depleting oxygen faster than your blood can deliver it; as a result, they turn to *anaerobic metabolism*, which uses carbohydrates in the form of glucose and glycogen to fuel the action of your muscles. This process creates a buildup of lactic acid that causes a burning feeling in your arms and legs.

This burning feeling slows you down considerably, and the champ uses the opportunity to land a series of blows to your head. Adrenaline keeps you from feeling most of the pain, but your brain is reeling from the attack. Whenever you're struck in the head, the velocity of the blow causes your skull to move away from impact—but your brain remains still and literally rattles against the inside of your head. This causes small patches of trauma inside your brain and reduces the blood flow throughout your head.

You are feeling very woozy. Another solid punch sends you down, and the limited blood flow causes you to fall momentarily unconscious. The crowd and the ring drift away, and when you come to, the referee is standing over you and shouting, "Seven! Eight! Nine! Ten!" You stagger to your feet, but the bout is over—and not a moment too soon. The crowd erupts with cheers, jeers, and applause. Someone in the front row shouts, "You cost me ten grand, you bum!" Even the pay-per-view cameramen are shaking their heads, as if wondering how such a lame fight could possibly be worth $49.95.

The champ hoists the championship belt above his head, and you wonder how he manages the strength; right about now, you can barely lift your arms to your face. Your trainers lead you back to the dressing room where you collapse on the table. The adrenaline is wearing off and the pain is setting in. Your body will ache for days, but you'll take some comfort in your guaranteed purse, which exceeds five million dollars. You might be a loser, but you make a great living.

shake, rattle, and roll over

I felt the car go upside down and turn around and then it came down and crashed. I felt the nose hit real hard. Then, I watched my hand break. That was weird. After that, I was unconscious.

—NASCAR DRIVER RUSTY WALLACE, ABOUT HIS CRASH IN THE 1993 WINSTON 500

Only two more laps to go—and with the leader in sight, you have a legitimate chance of winning your first Daytona 500. You try to remain focused, holding back and waiting for the perfect moment to make your move. Of course, you're also conscious of the forty-one other drivers behind you, all trying their hardest to creep up to the front of the pack.

For half a lap, you remain within striking distance, racing along "in the draft" (this is basically an extreme form of tailgating—you're riding nose-to-tail behind other cars to reduce wind resistance on your own vehicle). One of the oval's four large turns is coming up fast—so you downshift your vehicle and ease into the turn. You handle it perfectly, keeping the car parallel to the sides of the track and making sure your rear tires don't spin out too much. Up ahead, the lead car fishtails slightly, heading toward the outside wall. This is the opportunity you've been waiting for: You shift, press down on the accelerator, and make your move.

Unfortunately, the driver behind you has the same idea, and as his vehicle surges forward, he bumps you from behind. It's just a nudge, but when you're hurtling around a racetrack at nearly two hundred miles per hour, even the slightest disturbance is critical. Your car spins off to the right, slowing your forward momentum; you don't need to look in the rearview mirror to know that a collision is imminent. "This is gonna hur—" you say out loud, just before the impact smashes you from behind.

When 3,000-pound stock cars with custom-built 725-horsepower engines fly around a racetrack at breakneck speeds, spectacular crashes are inevitable. In fact, there are an average of three crashes at every NASCAR event, and more than one hundred wrecks during a typical thirty-two-race schedule. It sounds bad, but when you consider that 1,500 entrants are traveling more than 500,000 miles at speeds approaching two hundred miles per hour, it's surprising that the number of wrecks isn't higher. Even more surprising is that most drivers walk away from a wreck with nary a scratch. Sometimes they'll even finish the race after hopping in a "backup car."

Since 1952, there have been only thirty fatalities in sanctioned NASCAR races, but that's enough for the rule book to include a rather ominous warning: "The risk of serious injury or death cannot be eliminated and, in fact, will always be present at a high level. Members are required to advise their spouses and next of kin, if any, of this fact." Your family is definitely aware of these risks—and they're not happy about any of them.

But you don't become a racecar driver if you don't thrive in this environment, snacking on the speed and inherent danger. Besides, you know that countless precautions are taken to protect the drivers. For all their speed and power, stock cars are built like miniature tanks. Under their sheet metal exterior (not very different from the outer layer of a Ford Taurus), there is a complex frame of steel tubing designed to collapse and absorb impact. The center section of the car is much stronger and is built to maintain its shape. You are encased in a web of one-eighth-inch-thick steel tubes, and your body is restrained in a contoured, metal-backed seat with the help of a five-point seatbelt system—it has two straps across your waist, two over your shoulders and one between your legs. Finally, the windows of your car are covered with a nylon webbing which, in the event of a crash, should keep your limbs inside the vehicle (and flying debris *out* of the vehicle).

You wear a full face helmet; it is padded on the inside, and its visor is made of the same material as bullet proof glass (so is your windshield, for that matter). Your racesuit is also a surprisingly sophisticated work of engineering. At first glance, it simply resembles a walking billboard; the chest, back, and sleeve are covered with Alpo dog food logos. But underneath all the flashy advertisements is a special flame-resistant material that will protect you in the event of an explosion; your gloves, socks, and shoes are made from the same substance.

Up until your tiny nudge from Car #17, your performance at the Daytona 500 had been nothing less than superb. After your 237th lap, you pulled out of the pit road with new tires and a renewed confidence, knowing that you were heading into the final few laps as one of the leaders. You got your car in gear and returned to the pack. Everything was going well and you were locked in. But then came that bump from behind.

Suddenly your vehicle is perpendicular to the oncoming traffic. You're hit again, but this time it's not a nudge. A racecar collides with the left rear of your vehicle; your body jerks forward, and you feel as if you're airborne.

You crash down again and hear the clamorous sound of metal scraping asphalt. Sparks rain down outside your open window, and then you smash into the concrete sidewall. Your head snaps forward and back, the muscles hyperextending, and your spine comes dangerously close to snapping from the base of your skull. The screeching noise subsides as your car slows and stops. Soon you're aware of nothing but the sound of your own breathing. For the first time in weeks, tens of thousands of rowdy NASCAR spectators have suddenly fallen silent.

Your car flipped, smashed into the sidewall, and then traveled upside down off the track and onto the grass. But you don't realize any of this; you're still bracing yourself, expecting that further collisions are imminent, that the cars will keep crashing into a huge multivehicle pileup. When that doesn't happen, you manage to take stock of your situation; you're suspended upside down in your chair, and now the crumpled top of your vehicle is about six inches from the gearshift knob. You release yourself from the five-point belt system and remove the webbing from your window. As soon as you see the green grass, you realize you're safe—for the moment. You wriggle through the window and pull yourself out of the car.

While you're still emerging, the rescue crew is running up with their fire extinguishers, and they spray your car just in case. Paramedics are also rushing to attend to you; the first one screams, "Are you okay? Can you breathe?"

Lying in the grass, you feel like you've been pounded with a hundred hammers, and you can't move your right arm (your clavicle snapped like a twig as your body whipped against the safety belt). But otherwise, the worst of your damages are some nasty bruises. "I'm okay, I'm fine," you tell him, and then wave and call out to your friends in the pit crew: "Hey, somebody bring me the back-up car!"

the 12,000-foot-high jump

It's fantastic; you have no frame of reference, so it doesn't feel like you are falling more than 100 miles an hour. You just spin, and the wind is incredible.

—JOHN ISON, FIRST-TIME SKYDIVER, SARATOGA, CALIFORNIA, 1999

You inch toward the open door of the airplane, where your instructor, Jane, is waiting for you to join her. The other passengers are cheering you on, but you know they're just relieved it's not their turn. Jane reminds you to grab the strut hard with one hand, and directs you to place one foot on the rail outside. You get your first glimpse of the expanse of blue sky and the ground very far below. The wind is roaring in your face. Your heart is pounding, and for a brief moment you think about backing out. But when Jane taps you on your shoulder, you know you're hooked in. There's no turning back now—Jane yells "Go!"

and you do something you never thought you'd ever do: You leap from an airplane 12,000 feet above the earth.

Skydiving is no longer just an extreme sport for daredevil adrenaline junkies. It's actually become a fairly commonplace recreational activity, and more than five million jumps are made each year. But that regularity doesn't make it any less dangerous. It is still, after all, jumping out of an airplane, and even with every precaution and training available, accidents can happen: On average, there are thirty fatal skydiving accidents per year. But even with those deaths, it's safer than scuba diving, and more people will die from drinking bad tap water. The most dangerous part of the trip is driving to the launch area.

The possibility of a parachute not opening—every beginner's first concern—is basically nonexistent. Each jump is made with two parachutes, a primary and backup. The easiest way for a novice to dive with little training is to participate in a tandem dive. In this setup, the neophyte is attached by harness to the expert diver, who is then attached to the chute. No extensive training or certification is required—in one afternoon, a person can plunk down about two hundred dollars and experience the ultimate rush.

When your boss first proposed the idea, you hoped he was joking. It sounded like one of those "let's-all-bond-by-almost-dying" retreats that are so in vogue. But you don't want to die with these people. You don't even like sharing a bathroom with them. In the end, however, your opinion doesn't count for very much. When you told your boss you'd be happy to stay at the office and work on a spreadsheet, he gave you such a withering look that you ran out of your cubicle and jumped on the bus. Soon, your whole company was on its way to a rural stretch of farmland in eastern Pennsylvania.

You arrive at a runway with a tiny little Cessna and an airplane hangar. The first thing you have to do is read and sign about seventeen pages of waivers. You hesitate when you see words like *hazardous*, *injury*, and *death*, but your boss is standing over your shoulder, nudging you along. "It's just boilerplate," he assures everyone. "Let's go, people!"

Your next stop is a small conference room inside the hangar, where you and your coworkers watch a short video about tandem skydiving.

At the end of the video, a lawyer appears on the screen to remind you once again about the risks of skydiving. You don't like lawyers much to begin with, and this one uses words like *dismemberment, paralysis, multiple fractures,* and *at your own risk.* Your boss is drumming his fingers on the tabletop. "Yadda, yadda, yadda," he says. "When do we suit up?"

Your instructor and tandem partner, Jane, assures you that she has performed dives with more than 3,000 first-timers just like yourself. She reviews the equipment and explains some fundamental information: how to exit the aircraft, how to position your body, and how to operate the parachute system—including the backup chute, which is designed to open automatically if something goes wrong. During your training, you find it hard to concentrate. You're literally shaking with nervous anticipation as your heart beats faster and your blood pressure rises. All of your coworkers have the same kind of fake nervous smiles, and you can't help but wonder if your stock options are really worth all of this.

The instructions last only thirty minutes, and then it's time to get dressed. You don the all-important harness, which is made of heavy nylon straps and a series of metal rings. As you walk across the runway, approaching the airplane, your boss leads your coworkers in chanting the office cheer: "Who's the best?" "*We're* the best!" "Who tries harder?" "*We* try harder!" You feel like you're going to puke.

Once you're seated on the plane, Jane explains that anyone who wants to abort the dive just has to say so. Your boss mumbles something under his breath that sounds like "mamby-pamby bullshit" but no one else seems to hear it. The Cessna noisily takes off and you are on your way. You finally begin to calm down and try to block any nervous thoughts from your mind. As you focus on the roar of the engine, your heartbeat slows to a more normal rate for the first time all morning.

The plane climbs to about 7,000 feet and you put on your goggles. Jane motions to you and you kneel as she attaches her harness to yours, cinching the cords tightly. At 12,000 feet Jane makes her way toward the airplane door. She looks back and gives you a thumbs-up. You get up and wordlessly follow her lead. You are afraid to look out below for fear of vertigo, but you do look, and the distant nondescript ground looks less menacing than you would have imagined. You get in position and then you are in the air.

The first few seconds are the weirdest. The wind is fierce and very cold at this altitude, something you hadn't anticipated. You are very disoriented and not really aware of where you are—a combination of your nerves and the unique sensation of free fall. When you first leave the plane, your body is moving at the same speed as the plane, about 80 miles per hour. But you quickly accelerate in the first nine seconds of your dive and reach what is called *terminal velocity*. This is a constant speed at which the wind resistance is equal to your mass. You feel like you're floating, but in actuality, you are falling to the ground at a speed of 120 miles per hour. Expert divers can alter their body position for increased or decreased surface area to control their rate of descent; by doing so, many can reach speeds of 200 miles per hour and up.

You're so nervous, you're holding your breath—but if you wanted to, breathing would be quite simple. You cannot hear any sound but the roar of the wind in your ears. Thirty-five seconds after jumping, just as you are getting used to the fall, Jane yells for you to pull the ripcord, and you do. There is a slight jerk of tension, and your speed of descent slows to about twenty miles per hour. With the absence of the wind noise, it is now eerily quiet. Jane signals to you to use the two handles at your side to direct your fall. As you drift to the ground, you finally regain all your senses. The experience is remarkably tranquil—nothing but an expanse of clear blue sky and the ground below, which still looks very far away but is quickly coming into focus.

You're more relaxed than you would have ever imagined and taking regular breaths again. The quiet is broken by the emerging sounds of cars and people below. You are closing in on a field where the prearranged drop zone is located. With Jane's help, you make a gentle landing—on your feet no less!—and your chute trails colorfully behind. Your coworkers follow, dropping out of the sky with their tandem partners on their backs.

Your boss hits the ground last, collapsing with a thud and flailing in the folds of his chute. He sees you and your coworkers laughing and shouts, "You're all fired!" The funny thing is, he's probably not kidding.

don't forget your launch!

Eight minutes into the flight, we were pulling seven and a half Gs, grunting to expand our lungs against the incredible pressure.

—*GEMINI* ASTRONAUT EUGENE CERNAN, IN HIS BOOK *THE LAST MAN ON THE MOON*, 1999

The first thing you notice is just how tiny the *Gemini* spacecraft is. Yes, you've been training in simulators for months, but it's not until launch day, when you climb into the real thing, that the vessel feels so confining. The year is 1965 and the first moon walk is still a few years away, but the pedal-to-the-medal space race is here and now. For the next three days, you and your copilot will orbit the earth in a small vessel that's tinier than a Volkswagen. You'll have to lie on your back for the duration of the trip, looking straight up out of a tiny window into the cosmos. Just before liftoff, the cabin is filled with an eerie silence. Your copilot, John, must be as nervous as you—he's certainly just as quiet. All you hear is a low buzz, the crackle of the radio in your space helmet, and the slight hiss of oxygen being pumped into your space suit. The oxygen smells clean, crisp, and vaguely antiseptic.

Here you are, about to experience something that only a handful of humans have: the sensation of leaving and reentering the earth's atmosphere. (In fact, you have a much greater chance of becoming a rock star than an astronaut.) All the pretest flight checks have been performed and there's nothing left to do but wait. The voice of mission control on the other end of that radio cuts the silence and offers an ingenuous "Good luck, guys." The same voice then begins the countdown (10-9-8-7-6-5-4-3-2-1), and the huge rocket stretching underneath you starts to fire.

You look at John and he gives you an emphatic thumbs-up sign. The rocket is twenty stories high and there's a noticeable shudder as the fuel is ignited. You feel a slight bump as the bolts holding you to the launch tower explode, releasing the rocket. You slowly start to ascend as the rocket rumbles underneath you. Wispy white clouds move swiftly past your small window, and you're pushed back in your seat, like you're taking off in a commercial airliner. Then suddenly the clouds are gone from sight, and the force pushing you back in your seat increases.

The slow movement gives way to a much greater leap of speed. In your headset, mission control informs you, "Everything is good to go." The force builds on your chest like the weight of a pile of cinder blocks. You grit your teeth against the mounting Gs. (Acceleration is measured in terms of *G-force*, one G being the pull of Earth's gravity on the surface.) While training, you were subjected to eight Gs, but the simulators never quite captured the intensity of the real thing. As your speed increases, the force on your body increases, and you have more and more difficulty breathing.

There's a loud thundering noise and the craft shakes violently, making your whole body quiver like a bowl of Jell-O. Your eyes can't focus on anything and the instrument panel appears blurry. After just two minutes into your journey, you're already feeling about five Gs of pressure, which is the amount of force generated by the Titan rocket that is propelling you out of the Earth's atmosphere.

By this point, the first stage rockets are running out of fuel—but this is actually a cause for relief, not panic. As the last of the fuel burns away, the Gs suddenly disappear—and it's like you're braking in a speeding car. The momentum sends your body crashing forward against the heavy restraining straps. Exhaust from the rocket's burn is moving forward with the same, unchecked motion, and your craft is briefly engulfed in an orange and yellow fireball. The first stage rocket is now extinguished, and you have a moment to catch your breath.

But it's just a moment. The second stage rocket is already firing, and the pressure steadily increases until you reach a high of seven Gs. You struggle to expand your chest, desperate to get an adequate amount of oxygen into your lungs—and from the grunts of your copilot, you know that John is struggling, too. The second stage rocket burn lasts a few more minutes—but once you reach your intended orbit, the rocket separates from your tiny *Gemini* module with a shudder.

You are in space. You immediately forget how strenuous and uncomfortable takeoff was, and simply smile at the realization that you're actually drifting through our solar system. Outside your small glass window is a magnificent view of the bright blue planet below. Inside the cabin, you're completely weightless, and every now and then a tiny flake of debris will drift past the visor of your space helmet. You can't believe you've made it this far.

The mission lasts three days and you circle Earth forty-five times. While in space, you perform a number of experiments (the most important one involves docking with a previously launched spacecraft). You and John also perform a number of unauthorized experiments, most of which involve weightlessness, NASA-supplied rations, and anything else you can try to fling at each other. You're both in high spirits because the mission has been a success—but you know that it's far from over.

Any astronaut will tell you that reentry is the real kick in the rear. When mission control provides the signal, you fire a series of retro rockets that slow your movement, which allows the earth's gravitational pull to bring you back home. After three days of living in zero gravity, the force of the rockets hits you like a freight train, slamming you back in your chair. For a few minutes, you're simply speechless. But the burn is quick, and soon the ship is slow enough to be absorbed by the gravitational pull. At this point, you begin what is basically a free fall.

The retro rockets are jettisoned, exposing the all-important heat shield that will absorb the friction between the craft and the earth's atmosphere. The shield is on the back of the small craft, and you are now facing skyward, on your back, but at an angle so the horizon of Earth is visible in the upper portion of the cabin window.

As you enter the Earth's upper atmosphere, a sheath of ionized gas surrounds the spaceship and makes radio communication with mission control impossible. Someone calls out "Have a safe trip" just before you lose contact, and John mutters a string of obscenities. The ship is accelerating quickly and you're both scared as hell.

Fortunately, the heat shield appears to be working—bright fiery streaks pass by your window, which indicates that you're approaching the Earth's atmosphere. After a few more moments, these streaks culminate in a giant fireball that envelopes your ship. Despite the effectiveness of your shield, the temperature in the cabin rises to nearly 120 degrees. Sweat drips off your face and lands on the face plate of your space helmet. The pressure also increases to about five Gs as you continue re-entry, and soon you start to feel a nasty series of bumps.

The Earth's upper atmosphere is made of corrugated layers of molecules; as your craft descends toward the planet, you bounce from ridge to ridge of this atmosphere, like you're driving on an unpaved road. You try to ignore the bumps and simply stare out your window, where the collision between spacecraft and atmosphere is generating a pretty brilliant light show. It begins like an orange haze, grows brighter, and then darkens into a beautiful deep green.

When the flames finally fade, you deploy a small parachute to slow your descent to the ocean, and the craft wobbles from side to side. At about 16,000 feet, the main chute is deployed, and your view of the sky is obscured by the red-and-white material (the pattern makes it easy for NASA to determine your location). Your spacecraft smashes into the Pacific and you float on the surface of the ocean. The air of the cabin is filled with the faint smell of chemicals. A white seagull glides past your window. It feels good to be home.

BIBLIOGRAPHY

Ashcroft, Frances M. *Life at the Extremes*. Berkeley: University of California Press, 2000.

The Bantam Medical Dictionary. New York: Bantam Books, 1981.

Bjerklie, David, and Scott Norvell. "Ants in Our Pants: Forget Killer Bees. Here's a Bug from South of the Border That's Even More Frightening." *Time*, 5 June 1995.

Bondeson, Jan. *Buried Alive: The Terrifying History of Our Most Primal Fear*. New York: W. W. Norton, 2001.

Brown, Jeremy. "An Invisible Fire." *Discover*, April 1996.

Brownlee, Shannon. "Jellyfish Aren't Out to Get Us." *Discover*, August 1987.

Bryson, Bill. *A Walk in the Woods*. New York: Broadway Books, 1998.

Cernan, Eugene. *The Last Man on the Moon: Astronaut Eugene Cernan and America's Race in Space*. New York: St. Martin's Press, 1999.

Chiarella, Tom. "Stranded in Midstream: Kidney Stones." *Esquire*, September 1997.

Chowdhury, Bernie. *The Last Dive: A Father and Son's Fatal Descent into the Ocean's Depths*. New York: HarperCollins, 2000.

Collins, Michael. *Carrying the Fire*. New York: Farrar, Straus and Giroux, 1974.

Cowley, Geoffrey. "Cannibals to Cows: The Path of a Deadly Disease." *Newsweek*, 12 March 2001.

Dickens, Charles. *American Notes and Pictures from Italy*. New Oxford Illustrated Dickens. New York: Oxford University Press, 1957.

Fraser, Colin. *The Avalanche Enigma*. Chicago: Rand McNally, 1966.

Innes, Brian. *The History of Torture*. New York: St. Martin's Press, 1998.

Jenkins, McKay. *The White Death: Tragedy and Heroism in an Avalanche Zone*. New York: Random House, 2000.

Johnson, Robert. *Death Work*. Redmond, California: Wadsworth, 1990.

Laskin, David. *Braving the Elements: The Stormy History of American Weather*. New York: Anchor Books, 1996.

Le Vay, David. *Human Anatomy and Physiology*. Chicago: Hodder and Stoughton, 1988.

Max, D. T. "To Sleep No More." *New York Times Magazine*, 6 May 2001.

McGowan, Christopher. *The Raptor and the Lamb: Predators and Prey in the Living World*. New York: Henry Holt and Company, 1997.

McMillion, Scott. *Mark of the Grizzly*. Helena, Montana: Falcon Publishing, 1998.

Murphy, John C., and Robert W. Henderson. *Tales of Giant Snakes: A Historical Natural History of Anacondas and Pythons*. Malabar, Florida: Krieger Publishing Co., 1997.

Nagai, Takashi. *We of Nagasaki: The Story of Survivors in an Atomic Wasteland*. New York: Duell, Sloan and Pearce, 1958.

Nuland, Sherwin B. *How We Die: Reflections on Life's Final Chapter*. New York: Vintage Books, 1995.

O'Hanlon, Redmond. *In Trouble Again*. New York: Vintage Books, 1990.

Olsen, Jack. *Night of the Grizzlies*. New York: Putnam, 1969.

O'Reilly, James, Larry Habegger, and Sean O'Reilly, eds. *Danger! True Stories of Trouble and Survival*. San Francisco: Travelers' Tales, 1999.

Phillips, David. "How Frostbite Performs Its Misery." *Canadian Geographic*, 11 January 1995.

Poe, Edgar Allan. *The Poe Reader*. New York: State Street Press, 2000.

Preston, Richard. *The Hot Zone*. New York: Random House, 1994.

Robertson, Ian. "How Alcohol Works on Our Brains." *Times* (London), 20 December 1994.

Scaling Kiley, Deborah, and Meg Noonan. *Albatross: The True Story of a Woman's Survival at Sea*. Boston: Houghton Mifflin, 1994.

Schleser, David M. *Piranhas*. New York: Barron's Educational Series, 1997.

Selzer, Richard. *Raising the Dead: A Doctor's Encounter with His Own Mortality*. Knoxville, Tennessee: Grand Rounds Press, 1993.

Simon, David. *Homicide: A Year on the Killing Streets*. Boston: Houghton Mifflin, 1991.

Steel, Rodney. *Sharks of the World*. New York: Sterling Publishing Co., 1998.

Timmermans, Stefan. *Sudden Death and the Myth of CPR*. Philadelphia: Temple University Press, 1999.

Vertosick, Frank T., Jr. *Why We Hurt: The Natural History of Pain*. New York: Harcourt, 2000.

Wall, Patrick. *Pain: The Science of Suffering*. New York: Columbia University Press, 2000.

Weisberg, Jacob. "This Is Your Death; Capital Punishment: What Really Happens." *The New Republic*, 1 July 1991.

ACKNOWLEDGMENTS

The author would like to thank the following people for their assistance, support, and inspiration: Mom, Dad, Deb, Rob and Isabel Lutz, Grandma Min, Marcia and Peter Chesler, John "I Want My Free Dinner" Sellers, Paul Litton, Bernie Su, Chris Bruno, Brett Martin, the invaluable Jason Rekulak, Bryn Ashburn, Dave Borgenicht, Sarah Noreika, Nancy Armstrong, Jennifer Shenk, everyone at Quirk Productions and Chronicle Books, Patrick Kim, Joshua Piven, Robert Ducas, Kelly Wardell, Jessica Resnick, Pat Casler, the New York Mets, Henry, and, of course, my first and best extreme encounter, Jessica Chesler.